Bemelmans'
ITALIAN
HOLIDAY

Bemelmans' ITALIAN HOLIDAY

Written and illustrated by Ludwig Bemelmans

with a Foreword by Ted Patrick

Houghton Mifflin Company Boston

The Riverside Press Cambridge

1961

The contents of this book have appeared,
in different form, in *Holiday* magazine.

Design by Ervine Metzl
Second Printing
Printed in the U.S.A.

CONTENTS

FOREWORD

Ludwig Bemelmans is probably the only living author who started his writing career by scribbling drawings all over the walls of a restaurant. The restaurant was the Hapsburg House at 313 East 55th Street in New York. The year was 1933.

At the age of sixteen, Ludwig had been sent to the United States by his family to learn the ways of American hotel tending at New York's late and lamented Ritz. The Bemelmans' were brewers in Bavaria and innkeepers in the Tirol and were among the early investors in the enterprises of Charles Ritz. He worked at the hotel for several years, but his real love was art and his desire to draw and paint tugged so hard at him that it tugged him right out of the Ritz into the life of a free-lance artist. Then he got the inspiration for Hapsburg House; but at the time the inspiration enveloped him he was in one of his impecunious periods—he has a way of alternating between periods of yacht owning and subway riding—so he induced some of his friends to produce the money with which Hapsburg was born. A house was rented; a chef was hired; the builders and suppliers went to work; and, most important of all, wallpaperers came in and covered the walls completely from street-floor entrance to fourth-floor private room with drawing paper. Bemelmans went to work gleefully with India ink, crayons, water colors and brushes. Every room was given a different motif and every inch of wallpaper was obliterated by the art of Bemelmans.

Hapsburg House opened, and, after a shaky start, became a crashing success. Its success was social, artistic, gastronomic—everything except financial. For Bemelmans decided that it was time to emerge from his latest impecunious period into one of yacht owning or its equivalent, and the profits were barely enough to sustain him and his host of friends in caviar, Romanée Conti, and Dom Perignon. So after a while the partners, the creator, and the money lenders decided they had had enough fun with their toy and sold it to professional restaurateurs who had the crass notion that a restaurant should be run as a business. But before this happened, and before Bemelmans departed, he met a woman who was to change his life, Miss May Massey, who was in charge of the children's book department for Viking Press in New York. She had become entranced with the Hapsburg House as a restaurant and particularly with the Bemelmans drawings which adorned the walls. She decided that here was one of the great talents for children's books and persuaded him to try one. He did, and produced an utterly charming book entitled *Hansi*. He did another children's book and then a very mature book indeed, called *My War With the United States*. Then followed the famous Madeleine books, novels (*The One I Love the Best*), plays

(*Now I Lay Me Down to Sleep*), and, inevitably, travel books. "Travel book" is said with a wince because it conjures a vision of guidebooks and stories of "My Trip." Bemelmans' books in the genre go vastly beyond this. It would be more accurate to call them books about places and people seen through new eyes, heard through new ears, expressed through new talents. And it was inevitable that he write such books because he is truly one of the few Citizens of the World.

Bemelmans brings a strange, unique, and enviable armament to his assault upon a locale, a city, a section or a country. He listens with the ears of a consummate writer and sees with the eyes of a brilliant artist. He has multiple ears and multiple tongues, for he understands and speaks, not in high school but in academy fashion, English, German, French, Italian and Spanish. He can be a natural and welcome companion of Madeleine and her friends, an understanding cohort of the decadent old general in *Now I Lay Me Down to Sleep,* a rollicking fellow roué of the unconscionable Cucuface in *How to Travel Incognito.* He is accepted in a raffish bistro in Les Halles or at an elegant *Ballo in Maschera* on the Grand Canal in Venice.

This book has to do with Italy. All of the material first appeared in *Holiday,* to which Bemelmans has been for years a consistent contributor. It is a joyful day when one of his manuscripts, such as those which appear on the following pages, arrives in the *Holiday* office. It is an equally joyful day when the drawings and paintings to accompany the manuscript arrive. In this book you will get a new insight into many of the lovely places of Italy—Venice, Rome, the Italian Riviera, Naples, Capri and Ischia. But more important, you will meet people, the old prince in the

Borghese Gardens of Rome, the sunny girl who did the chores in Bemelmans' rented villa in Capri, and the professor in exile in Ischia, the wonderful island that for so long has languished in the shadow of glittering Capri. These are not characters of fiction, they are real people; and by bringing them and the others to you vividly, Bemelmans makes Italy itself more real, perhaps, than any book on Italy has ever done before.

Ted Patrick

Philadelphia
1961

MAGIC ROME

Rome

PUROR HIC AER LA

Rome

On the two hours' trip between London and Rome, the jet barely attains operating height when it has to start the descent. The Mediterranean appears, and an ocher-colored landscape. The sign flashes on: *Fasten your seat belt—No smoking please.* You see it briefly as if a dealer of art prints showed you a picture and took it away. Then, like a bobsled on the Cresta Run, you come to land. When you have put out your cigarette, Rome is below in a harmony of color. There before you are the clay tones of the most serene city in the world: the sad yellow of a malarial patient, the pale hues of a sheep's pelt, all the shadings of sunbaked earth through the umbers and burnt siennas up to the old rose of ancient brick; and this is all festooned with white marble, gold and the dark green of pines and cypresses, the pale emerald green of the Tiber.

Those who get off here "pass through" like a letter through the mail, as the French say. I went out to a car. I had no Italian currency, so I asked the driver of a taxi to pay the porter. I said that I would pay him at the hotel.

"How much, signore?"

"Give him a good tip."

"And what is a good tip?" He made gestures illustrating the hopelessness of arriving at a decision.

"All right," I said, "what do you consider a good tip for carrying a bag weighing twenty-two and a half kilos—about one hundred meters?"

"Ah, signore," said the chauffeur, "who can tell? You are the one to decide."

"Good," I said, "then give him one lira." There are around 620 lire to the dollar, at the present exchange. There was some rapid action, the bag was in the cab, and the chauffeur decided that 200 lire was a fair tip. We started for Rome.

Don't complain if the clerk in any of the grand hotels in Rome gives you a bad room. In Rome a bad room is usually good because it is at the back of the house or facing on a courtyard. It is shady and it is quiet. The best rooms face the avenues and are the noisiest in the world.

In Italy all people are motor-crazy. One who cannot afford a car buys a motor-scooter. The motorscooter is marketed by the thousands. The Vespa is the noisiest. When far away it has the sound of a wasp, but as it roars up the Via Veneto it changes to that of a regiment on machine-gun practice. On that account, get a cheap, inside room. I stayed at the Hotel Excelsior. This is a first-rate establishment—efficient, clean and international.

The lobby of the Hotel Excelsior is like the lobby of the George V in Paris or the Savoy in London—the same baggage—the same people—except here and there a Father O'Reilly on a pilgrimage—I sat there waiting for a friend, an Italian artist who spent years in New York.

As I waited, Fulton J. Sheen, Prince of the Church, wandered back and forth in the elegant lobby with a lovely Roman woman. There were several Hollywood producers, all of whom knew the Bishop and nodded to him, and he smiled back. In a nest of easy chairs next to me were some English people. They were waiting for someone who presently arrived, an Italian, and they said, "Oh, we have some really nice Americans who've taken the house for the summer, and that's how we can afoohd to be heah." And suddenly my friend Paolo came forward in dramatic fashion and embraced several people. Finally he saw me and said, "Ah, *caro*—so you're back in Rome. What a privilege for you to be able to come here every year." Paolo is, as most Romans are, bored by anything that does not happen in Rome.

Paolo is poor, like most artists. He is small, a cock sparrow of a man, with a fierce pride. He never accepts an invitation to a meal without returning it.

"The last time," he said, "you invited me. This time I invite you."

Also, he takes you only to the best places. So we went to Passetto's. He ordered wine and some little birds. He insisted on paying. When you come from France you are surprised at the Italian prices, which are about half as high as those in France.

There is a buffet at Passetto's, an exhibition of food some eight feet wide and twelve feet high, nicely arranged, and everything on it is recommendable, although Paolo refuses to eat the mussels, oysters or clams. Having been made ill years ago by bad oysters, he is convinced that all bivalves are polluted.

Paolo says the same is true of Roman society. "*Caro*, we have here the most venomous gossip in the world. In other places they talk meanly about people, but here they talk murderously. There are three kinds of society here—dull, duller and dullest, in that order, going toward the top. Descendants of eleventh century Romans consider anyone later a parvenu. A complete atrophy is in the palaces, and most of the aristocracy detest the Americans. There are some exceptions who imitate them. You see that average-looking business type sitting there? He is a count, but not of the eleventh century. He tries to be more American than Henry Ford; he has great projects for improving the lot of his workers, for industrializing his territory—he is called a communist . . . That beautiful American blonde over there is married to the chap with her. He has a farm near Florence and is also a count. He is not the usual run of young man, although you can see he is extremely good-looking. He is not a dope addict, a runner after skirts or wrecker of racing cars. He works—which is considered disgraceful. Besides, he is trying to help his field workers, and it was reported with shudders that he even shakes hands with them and puts electric light in their huts.

"Society here is mummified, and individual samples of it are like petrified wood cut across the grain, beautifully polished, lying on glass shelves in a museum—and just as cold to the touch. And if they were to bend, they'd break.

"Oh, yes—the Romans were disturbed because Clare Luce came as U.S. Ambassador. Being an Ambassador, she was technically a man—ergo—you could not kiss her hand, but—being an Ambassador, she was decorated—ergo—you had to kiss her cheek as you pinned the orders on her. This threw the diplomats into confusion. When she arrived, a local magazine printed a picture of the U.S. flag edged with the lace of ladies' underthings. If it bothered them so much, why didn't they make Anna Magnani Italian Ambassador to Washington?

"There is one more thing. Out at the golf club near the Appian Way a revolution is going on. One faction wants to throw out all the Americans, and the other wants to keep them in because they pay their dues and all the bills too. Now I have told you all that is new in Rome, which is nothing—one mediocre night club. It is the most beautiful city in the world, it has a marvelous climate, but there is nothing exciting unless you love antiquity, music, statuary, gardens and religion."

As on every visit, I went to St. Peter's the next morning with Paolo to look at the Pietà of Michelangelo. Paolo stopped at St. Peter's statue—he is a devout Catholic—and, as Italians do, he kissed the toe of the saint, which is worn flat with kisses.

Paolo has a peculiar way of kissing it. He plants his kiss on the tip of the index finger of his right hand and touches the toe with it.

Paolo looked at me as he wiped his finger on a snow-white handkerchief. "You come here every time and yet you are not religious."

I said, "I wish I was."

"Oh, I am glad to hear you say that. I don't mind, *caro*, that you are not. You can doubt religion, you can get angry at it, you can amuse yourself with the priests, God knows not all of them are serious. But you cannot dismiss lightly or ridicule the believer. To take religion from anyone I think is criminal—what can you give them instead?"

The next day I asked Paolo to take me to some medium-priced restaurants that the tourist would like. We went to a place called Al Re delgi Amici, in the Via della Croce. The table next to us was occupied by a blind man with a Seeing Eye dog. The dog was nervous. The man kicked it to make it get under the small table, then kicked it again, harder. The waiter tried to feed the dog, which was skinny. The man told him that the dog was properly fed at home. The blind man wore a long cape and spoke in Neapolitan dialect.

I said to Paolo, in English, "If that dog has any sense, he'll lead that bastard under the first big bus that comes down the Via Veneto."

Paolo said, "I hope the dog understands English."

The blind man turned his face toward us and said: "The dog doesn't understand English, but I do." He paid and left.

Besides Al Re delgi Amici, I can recommend Neroni, Nino's, Romolus, Peperil, Gerretezzi, all of them good, and all inexpensive. If you get tired of spaghetti, there is the Piccolo Budapest for Hungarian food, and the Viennese Tavern with good sausages and sauerkraut which is called *krauti* in Italy; the beer there is good too.

The important thing for the fashionable traveler to remember about Rome is that no one who is anybody is ever seen there in August. The gardens of the Villa Borghese tremble in heat, the carriage horses can hardly hold up their heads. Crossing a street wilts you and not even the shadows of St. Peter's offer relief.

6 Winter can be cold, but then there are very good furs to be had. In the shops along the Via Condotti you can also buy the world's most fabulous jewels, exquisite shoes, shirts, gowns. The outstanding characteristic here is that the salespeople are cooperative; they work with almost magic speed. They take your measurements for shirts, for example, and then ask when you need them. You say: "Tomorrow morning." They are at your hotel the next morning—and they fit. A little more time, understandably, is needed for suits and gowns.

The manners of the *couturiers* here are those of people who have attended a good kindergarten. The clientele is always treated with civility. The same is true of restaurants. In this city, which is the world's most magnificent cemetery, a great Italian restaurateur has stepped into his tomb. His name was Alfredo, and no visit to Rome was complete without having him mix *fettucini* for you in the restaurant that bears his name. He looked like the late King Vittorio Emanuele decorated with important mustachios. When all was ready for him, he was summoned to your table. From the breast pocket where most men keep a handkerchief he pulled a golden fork and spoon given to him by Douglas Fairbanks and Mary Pickford. With these he mixed the noodles in expert rhythm, a performance no less profound than when Toscanini conducted *La Forza del Destino*. Alas, others conduct and mix noodles—and trim poodles.

As beautiful as Rome is, to most of its orderly citizens it is as quiet as a village. "Nothing ever happens," they complain. There is no Folies Bergères, although musical comedies are tolerated.

But there is open-air opera in the Baths of Caracalla; concerts, races, tennis matches, and every form of approved amusement. And, as in most large European cities, there is also clandestine entertainment.

After a week I left, this time aboard the new Viscount, a turbo-jet plane. I said goodbye to Paolo at the airfield.

MIDAS TOUR OF ITALY

Now THAT the French have broken through the sound barrier and silenced the tooting of auto horns in Paris—a feat I never dared hope would come to pass—I wished it might be possible to stop the machine-gun blasts of the Roman scooters driving past the Hotel Excelsior with cutouts wide open. The racket was so penetrating that I could scarcely concentrate on the letter I had just been handed at the desk. It was from an acquaintance in Pittsburgh. He and some friends were coming to Italy. They wanted to see, he wrote, the places where the rich Italians went. Could I plan an itinerary?

It was a difficult request, since the rich man's Italy, as he thought of it, is a thing of the past, and today's ultrarich Italian arranges his most expensive splurges away from Italy.

I put the letter in my pocket and, leaving the staccato noises of the Via Veneto, walked up to the gardens of the Villa Borghese, my morning promenade. Here you are enfolded by classical statuary and botany. The morning sun silhouettes acanthus leaves, palms and laurel on the carefully raked walks; the wind swishes through the high umbrella pines, and lining the paths are rows of busts on pedestals. You can gaze into the faces of great men of the past, spaced like fence posts, all life size, serious and superbly executed. It has all grown together in a harmony of shape and color. The light is filtered, the stone is aged, the mood . . . eternal. It is, as is all Rome, the only place for which I feel nostalgia while I am there.

After passing the busts of Scipio, Baldo, Verdi, Ponzio and Cavour, one arrives at a water clock, an instrument the size of a telephone booth, set upon rocks. Its walls are of glass, and inside it there is a simple apparatus motivated by a thin stream of water which turns wheels that move the clock's hands. The rocks are moss-covered, the clock is oxidized, and beneath it is a pool where water lilies grow and goldfish swim; the water splashes in the tempo of a swinging pendulum, the goldfish gulp in the same measure—*blup, blup, blup*—and there is an ancient gardener who rakes the walk in cadence.

In this peaceful grove is a bench where now and then I meet a man of experience. His head well might be a model for statuary; his hands are elegant, his fingers long and thin. I sit with him often and talk. On this day I ask his advice on what Italian tour a rich man should take.

"Ah, the *ricchissimi* tour of Italy," he said, and shook his head. He patted his companion, an old dog named Pascal.

Ricchissimi means the superrich. Another word that often goes with the more elderly superrich is *gaga*, which denotes the happy state of mind that is a mellow mildew of the memory. It means, in a kind way, that one has slipped the harness of care. One in this state has a clarity of vision that has been filtered through the mesh of vanity and passion. He has the directness and the bright gaze of a child; and like a baby, he frequently drops off to sleep.

One of the nicest of the *gaga* is this ancient gentleman I meet in the gardens of the Villa Borghese. He used to be *ricchissimo*. Now he is poor—that is, he has only four servants and a solitary palace. He is Principe Bartolomeo Troiani. He has been everywhere and seen everything, for his passion once was travel. On our first meeting he said that he was sorry to receive me in a public park, no longer having his own; he consoled himself with the fact that the government, not he, was paying for keeping it neat.

He has a sensitive, joyful countenance; a shock of hair, a bold mustache and a pointed beard—all snowy white; he looks like a delicate Italian Buffalo Bill. He had been to America; in fact, he knew it well. And when I showed him my letter, he said, "Ah, Pittsburgh. I have friends there. Oh, the breathless pace of that city—the inexhaustible ambitions of its people." After he had said this he read the letter through, and there followed a reflective pause. "As for the *ricchissimi* tour of Italy," he said at last, "such a thing no longer exists—which makes it rather difficult." He raised his eyes slowly to the dial of the water clock, and then he said, looking down the path, "One of these mornings I shall introduce you to a man who knows everything about what's left of the rich man's Italy. He is the Duke of Fossombrone. He once had a shooting lodge in Scotland, establishments in London and Paris, a houseboat on the—what's the name of that river in India? Well, anyway, now he moves from his little house in Rome to a rented apartment at Torre Vajanica—the Coney Island of Rome. This is to create the illusion of going away, so that next winter he will be invited to the few remaining *palazzi;* no one who stays in Rome during the summer could be considered chic."

The Prince rested for a few minutes with eyes closed, then he asked what we had been talking about. "Oh, yes—the letter. This is a businessman from Pittsburgh— energetic and sports-loving, no doubt. Now the places that compare to Pittsburgh here are Torino, Milano and Genova. These places are filled with middle-aged *nouveaux riches.* They go to the Italian Riviera, called the Riviera dei Fiori because of the super-abundance of flowers. Not only do flowers grow outside but inside as well—in the hotels, in the post office, in every window. If you bleed here, it is probably from being scratched by a rose thorn.

"The most famous train serving the Riviera and the one preferred by the *nouveaux riches* is the train of the *Cornuti,* which means cuckolds. It runs from Genova, Torino and Milano to the Riviera dei Fiori. The cuckolds commute weekends to the Riviera where they are met by their wives. Stories say that the wives are driven to the station by companions who are with them during the week, and that after a last kiss, as the train whistle is heard, they disappear. The *Cornuti* stop and the manufacturers of salami, ships, textiles and automobiles detrain and clasp their spouses, for whose absence they have consoled themselves during the week. It is a very considerate arrangement and, except for the train ride, no one is ever lonely."

The Prince dropped off to sleep . . .

The Pittsburghs of Italy

Turin, Milan and Genoa have one thing in common—they are animated with commercial activity. They have hotels in which you will encounter people with briefcases rather than cameras. Architecturally, they have a slight French accent so that at times you think that you are walking down the Champs Elysées. At other times you think you have been transplanted back to America, for in the hearts of these cities the streets are at right angles and the office structures remind one of the musty solidity of downtown Philadelphia. And since I did not recommend these cities to my Pittsburgh friend, we will move on in search of a climate more Italian. We will take that excellent train recommended by the Prince to the Italian Riviera.

The Italian Riviera

There the lampposts along the promenades, of which there are many, are planted in beds of petunias. All season long, hotel doormen brush pollen from their uniforms. You eat flowers, wake up and go to bed with flowers. As in a perfume shop, you breathe their fragrance everywhere and if you bleed here, it is—as the Prince said—from the thorn of a rose someone has thrown at you during the frequent battles of flowers. The kitchens of hotels and private homes are influenced by the nearness of France. The Italian Riviera includes the seaside resorts of Alassio, San Remo and Bordighera, in which are comfortable family hotels, all facing the sea. The beach is gay with the costumes of nursemaids watching well-behaved children in large straw hats engaged in the serious business of building sand castles. This is a place for repose in deck chairs, good appetites satisfied by substantial meals, and early retiring. The signs in the corridors say that people are sleeping; no one here is eccentric. The train of the *Cornuti* arrives, filled to capacity, and the scenes of husbands and wives meeting are as genuinely matrimonial as anything observed in Suburbia, U.S.A.

On another morning, as the Prince and I sat in the Villa Borghese gardens, he lifted his hand slowly and waved it in greeting. "There comes the man with the proper qualifications—the one I told you about—who now goes for the summer to the Coney Island of Rome, but who once had two men in his household livery carry his moneybags into the Casino of Monte Carlo."

Deliberately the Duke of Fossombrone advanced. He was like a praying mantis—with a black cane—waiting among plants. His face was porcelain white, his hair jet black. The Prince introduced us and then asked the Duke where he would send Americans for a *ricchissimi* tour. The Duke traced the map of Italy in the sand with the ivory tip of his cane, and shrugged.

"Ah, *tempi passati!*" said the Duke, sadly. "I think Florence, Pisa and Siena are places one still can safely recommend. Of course, now one has to be very rich—more than *ricchissimo* in the Italian sense.

Florence

"In Florence I always stayed at the Grand Hotel. At that place lived a couple very much devoted—not to each other—to the hotel. They had come from Brazil more than twenty years before, and for the first ten years they shared a bedroom and salon. After that they asked for separate rooms. In another ten years, they drifted apart so that he was at the extreme end of their corridor and she at the other. They communicated by way of the maître d'hôtel in the dining room, where they were seated as far apart as possible. Both were attached to the hotel and, of course, to Florence. I wonder if they are still there."

On a Tour De Luxe one must be everywhere at the height of the season; therefore we find ourselves at the *Maggio Musicale* in Florence in May. Spring is the season for Florence. From Easter on, the hotels are filled, the restaurants crowded. The evening before Easter the cathedral is the scene of the pageant of the burning chariot, set aflame with holy fire. A vast wooden cart filled with fireworks and other combustible material, and decorated with flowers and ribbons, is drawn by two long-horned, snow-white oxen to the main portal of the cathedral.

At the altar inside, the Archbishop himself says High Mass—and above him is a small carved dove, suspended from a trolley wire. As the Archbishop says: "Glory to God in the Highest," he lights a wick in the mouth of the dove; the dove is pulled out of the building on the wire, the throngs outside shout with joy, and a moment later the chariot disintegrates. Sheaves of fireworks ascend into the sky, a barrage of explosions tears at your ears and everyone is in a state of elation.

Pisa

The neighboring city of Pisa leans on its tower for fame; 294 steps lead to the top, and the sufferer from vertigo should behold it from below. It is a curious sensation to look down from the leaning end, for now it leans over thirteen feet.

Siena

The annual Palio races take place in Siena during August and reservations must be made long in advance. The magnificent square of Siena is transformed into a racecourse, the preparations taking weeks, and the race is over in two minutes. It is the only race where a riderless horse may win. Pageantry, medieval flags thrown into the air and artfully caught, trumpets, and fifty-odd thousand people make this an exciting and exhausting spectacle. The rest of the year Siena is one of the most serene and beautiful of the cities of this region.

The gardener slowly raked his way toward where we sat, working backward. Now he turned around, pulled off his cap and in deep salute swept the ground with it. To the Prince he said, "Good morning, Most Noble Excellency," and made a slightly lesser reverence to the Duke. Weeks had passed, and again our meeting place was near the old water clock.

There is a way in which the true old Italian aristocrat can speak to a laborer as if he were addressing his brother, yet manage to maintain distance. "Alessandro," said the

Prince, with great friendliness, "if you had the choice, where would you go to spend
your vacation?"

The gardener leaned forward, making a tripod of himself and his rake. With his cap he waved in a southerly direction. "To my home, to Sicily, where the Americans have found oil—near Ragusa. One well alone gives over a thousand barrels a day. Perhaps we are rich."

"I hope it will come true, Alessandro," said the Prince. "But where would you take your family in the hot months if you were rich?"

The gardener, to whom this problem had never before been posed, looked worried, and finally he said, very humbly, "To the lakes, Your Most Noble Excellency."

The Italian Lakes

"Oh, yes, we forgot about the beautiful Italian lakes. Those who live in the past, like Prince Troiani, will tell you that the Italian lakes aren't what they once were. For example, the business of getting bronzed by the sun has become arduous. There was a time when each hotel on Lake Como had its own float offshore, and people who wanted to take the sun were propelled out to it in a gondola and brought back without suffering the shock of cold water.

"Things have changed now, and the younger generation dives off the high boards or swishes by on water skis. On the shores of Lake Como, Pliny, the Roman writer, built himself a villa, and he complained about the coldness of the water two thousand years ago. Actually, it is the temperature of the ocean at Atlantic City in July and August, but that is very grim bathing for Italians, who prefer underwater sports in the warm Mediterranean."

The gardener thought for a while, and then he observed, "The water seems very cold—it comes from the glaciers. Fortunately, we are not a passionately aquatic race, and limit ourselves to evening boat rides with guitars, mandolins and singing, and soft light from paper lampions. Then the lake is as beautiful as the silks that are spun along its shore in Como."

"What else is there with water?" asked the Prince.

"Venice," answered the gardener with enthusiasm.

Venice

Venice has impressed itself on the consciousness of people via the colored prints that hang in the waiting rooms of the world's dentists. When at last you see it, it is exactly so. You walk about it and you feel it. But, like all things rare and beautiful, it evades you, for it is a mirage. One wonders why this city which is like a thousand decorated barges floating in a lagoon, held together by small bridges, doesn't swim away or sink.

Most fascinating at night, the slow-moving dark waters are silvered with the wobbly reflections of marble bridges and stairways that lead down into them; water also laps at the doors of old palaces. The moon seems a Venetian lamp and the stars are like the little lights that flicker before the innumerable statues of the Madonna. As if a violin maker had turned his skill to the making of black coffins, the long, thin gondolas bob along. Wagner died in Venice, and Thomas Mann wrote *Death in Venice* here. It is, then, not a place to take one who is melancholy, for he will try to drown himself, and fail, for most of the canals are only four feet deep.

The streets of Venice haven't changed since the thirteenth century (a description of the city by Marco Polo could be used as guide today). There are shops of all kinds. Cigarettes of every make are available, and next to the glassware of Murano are gadgets made in the U.S.A.

There is no bad hotel in Venice—not even a tavern that will disappoint you. From the most luxurious, the Gritti Palace Hotel, to the humblest inn, the traveler is in hands as professional as those of the Swiss. Venice has a season the year round. In summer it is swamped with German tourists, most of them stalwart youths in buckskin trousers held up by embroidered leather braces, and blond companions in dirndls. Their elders come in large groups called *Reiserundfahrtsgesellschaften,* and to entertain them there are many *Bierstuben, Wurst* and *Kraut* dispensaries and *Schnitzelbänke* with singing.

The most beautiful month in Venice is September, when the city is crowded with international high society with its yachts, and with the world's film directors, producers and actors. Every room in Venice and on the Lido is taken. Lido means a bank—it is a sandbank that protects Venice from the waves of the sea. The water here is lukewarm and rises only twelve inches at high tide. The beach at the Lido is kind to the soles of your feet; it is soft and like clay. You can walk out into the sea for half a mile before it comes up to your hips.

Portofino

The Duke of Fossombrone and I chanced to meet outside my hotel one forenoon. Almost automatically we walked to the garden of the water clock, and there we found the Prince, asleep. The Duke said, "Ask him about his nephew, who surely knows where Americans would be happy. He is married to one."

"My nephew," mumbled the Prince, without opening his eyes. "Of course, why didn't we think of that before? Portofino—" The Prince raised a lid and looked at the water clock. "Will you gentlemen accompany me to my daily debauch of orange-flavored yoghurt? This little restaurant offers the most beautiful panorama of our Rome."

The Duke bowed agreeably, I nodded and slowly we proceeded down the alley lined with statuary and shaded by trees. Old Pascal came out from under the bench and followed the Prince at heel.

"My nephew, Count Rodolfo Troiani, is well off," said the Prince.

"*Very* well off," said the Duke.

"His wife is American—very pretty, but not exactly the girl of our choice." The Prince paused. "Rodolfo met her at Ciampino airport, where she had arrived as a member of an Irish American society to present the Holy Father with a gift.

"It was an official and very formal meeting. I am sorry to say that things became very informal after that. For example, she calls Rodolfo, Rudi—and my poor dog here, Pascal, she addresses as Buster."

"I'm sure they will like Portofino," said the Duke, bringing the conversation into line as we reached the restaurant.

We sat down and the Prince ordered his yoghurt. "Yes," he said, "Portofino is the best place. You know, this extraordinary girl has a passion for water skiing, and Rodolfo has to drive the motorboat that pulls her—an American motorboat—very fast. It's all bewildering to me. I saw them depart for Portofino once. She says 'Unk' to me, 'Goodbye, Unk—goodbye, Buster.' And then comes first a truck with the American motorboat on it. This is followed by a station wagon of American make, in which ride the count and countess; behind them are the baby and the nurse, and in back of them a harlequin great Dane. This is followed by an Italian Topolino into which are squeezed the count's *amministratore,* the chauffeur, the cook, the maid and all their luggage."

"Of all the small harbors," said the Duke, "that come close to what you Americans imagine them to be—small fishing towns untouched by modernity—the gem is Portofino. If you wanted to own a house anywhere in Italy, I would recommend that it be there. It has become a refuge for actors; you will find Rex Harrison and the Oliviers, in slacks and sweaters. There is a small bar but no night life, and one good hotel, the Splendido. Advise your friends not to go there without a reservation."

"The ideal way to go is by yacht," said the Prince. "In the small harbor there are as many foreign flags as one sees in Genoa. The boats are mostly seagoing, kept provisioned and ready to sail come the day of the revolution. You know, Ludovico, there is a real fear of communism among that class of Italians."

Taormina

"How about Taormina?" asked the Duke, getting up.

"Yes, very nice—beautiful in winter," said the Prince, who paid the check with carefully counted, dirty lire and left a small tip. "Everybody swims there except when it snows, but then you can ski on the slopes of Etna—unless you are afraid the volcano will erupt again."

"You see how hard it is," said the Duke, "to recommend places?"

"The answer is canasta," said the Prince. "All the fashionable world loves canasta—in Venice, in Portofino, in Taormina, in Palermo—and even here in Rome."

So I went to Sicily to see if Palermo and Taormina should be recommended. Of all the castles and abbeys that have been turned into hotels, the most agreeable that I have seen is the Dominican Convent hotel in Taormina. It is in the center of town, with a clear drop of a mile down to the sea on three sides. Its entrance is like that of a palace and the monks who retired to this place must have been of singular importance. The only things monkish about it are the doors of the cells which are so small that they barely admit a wardrobe trunk. But the cells themselves are roomy, each with a mag-

16   nificent view; the beds are comfortable and wide, the closets immense, and each cell has a bath. In the former robing room the bar is installed, and drinks are made on a refectory table.

Inside there is still a trace of incense in the air—outside you are anesthetized with the heavy fragrance of tropical flowers. The food is good, the coffee awful, the service is solicitude itself. The visitor can contemplate the beauty of the ancient Greek theater and the serene, snow-covered cone of Etna.

18   Below is a beach of black volcanic sands and bathing facilities which Italians use in July and August, Scandinavians from April on, and Americans and Germans all year.

If one wanders off into the village, he will see a lot of old women in black with one or —at most—three teeth; some younger ones in the costume of poverty, the faded dress that Lollobrigida wears in *Bread, Love and Dreams.* There are small boys smoking butts picked up in the elegant section up above. There are wild-looking kids who wear nothing but a castoff overcoat, and all of them have interesting faces—some look like dwarfed scientists, some like bankers and businessmen, but all have the faces of fighters. A few have something to sell, and they propose their deals as if a million dollars were at stake, and as if they were familiar with the intricate details of international commerce.

On the terraced hills one sees grapes; olive, orange and lemon trees; thin pigs, scrawny chickens, mangy cats—and on a fountain a tame crow with one leg, hopping to the edge to drink. And everyone here has a relative in America and thinks of it as Paradise . . .

Back in Rome I learned with regret that Prince Bartolomeo was ailing. The Duke of Fossombrone, however, was enjoying good health, and we met in a café of his suggestion for a drink. As we were served, a man so fat that he puffed when he breathed wobbled by us, accompanied by a companion who required two canes to make even the most painful progress. The Duke glanced from these gentlemen to me and said, "Ludovici, perhaps your American friends will need to take the cure at some of the watering places before they go home."

The Italian Spas

"There is Chianciano for the liver," the Duke went on, "Salsomaggiore for the kidneys, Abano for aching bones and arthritis. Another is Montecatini. At Abano you lie in hot mud and feel all dirty, but in contrast the waiters who bring your trays are in spotless uniforms; it is very chic. Once when I was there I observed true democracy. A very old American lady brought her ancient chauffeur and maid—they had been with her most of her life—and put them into the mud also."

We have eaten our way down the length of Italy from Piedmont and its *agnolotti* dishes of mixed boiled meats and its sauces called *fondua* and *bagna calda.* We have had *ossobuco,* a cut of the veal bone with saffron-colored rice which is the specialty of Milano. We've eaten the fish dishes and fish soups of Venice; the *pesto* sauce made of basil, olive oil and goat cheese. We've tasted the *tagliatelle* and *tortellini* and the great sausages of Bologna, *mortadella, cotechino* and salami, and its hams. We've stuffed ourselves on Tuscany's roast suckling pigs and the products of the Roman kitchen, the fried meats, the *fettucini,* the *bacalao* and deviled meats. In Naples we've had *pasta asciutta* and *pizza,* with the sauces which increase in fragrance and potency the farther south you go. We also have paid attention to the wines—the Chianti, Lacrima Christi, Barbaresco, Barbera, Soave, Orvieto, Verdiso—after all these pleasures of the stomach

CAPRI   THE
PIAZZA

it is time to see a doctor who will direct us to a pleasant retreat where the air, water and management combine to restore the victims of good food and to send them back with fresh appetites.

As the old Prince said, it is an awful responsibility to send someone anywhere. One of the great experiences of travel lies in taking upon yourself the risk of discovery. You may, unaccountably, turn into a crowded street—at the end of which, facing the most beautiful panorama you have seen, is a little hotel of which you have never heard, and which is perfect—and where even with a little car and a thin checkbook you are the *ricchissimo* traveler in the world.

DIARY WITH A BLANK PAGE

I AM never late for a train in Paris; in fact, the romantic scenery of a French railroad station attracts me even when I am not going anywhere. The pleasure of travel, for me, starts long before the train departs. I like to walk up and down the "quais," as the platforms from which trains leave are called, and watch the thousand things that go on —the farewells, the reunions, the embraces and tears, the gymnastics of the porters and the many details of travel. The conductors, some alert, some tired, the sleeping-car attendants, the cooks in the cramped quarters of the dining cars preparing meals—all this is set to the concert of the pumps of a dozen locomotives and the high yammering of the French train whistle; the sounds echo in the vast hall as in a mountain valley. The air is filled with carbon, and a soft blue light bathes the scene.

My grandfather once told me he could tell the character of a man by looking at his shoes. To me, a better index is his luggage. On the evening that I left for Rome, wandering up and down beside the train, I saw an exhibit of most luxurious luggage —twelve assorted bags of crocodile hide with heavy fittings and leather-framed tags. Under the supervision of the conductor and a man who seemed to be the valet of the owner of the bags, they were taken by porters into the sleeping car in which I had a compartment. At the last minute, as the conductor looked once more at his big reliable watch, the owner of the luggage arrived.

He was a nervous man, his legs and arms moving as if he were a marionettee. In contrast to his small, perpetually agitated limbs, his body was vast, like that of a bug. His head belonged neither to the limbs nor to the body, but looked like the head of a figure from a wax museum—artificial, with large, sad eyes. As he took his hat off and wiped his forehead, he exposed hair that was gray and stiff like a brush.

For years I have enjoyed a bowing, smiling acquaintance with him. He is at Cannes at the height of the season; he swims in an old-fashioned bathing suit at the Eden Roc. He walks in the snow at St. Moritz in plus fours and high shoes with the back straps sticking out, and wearing a pea-soup-colored jacket which he himself must have designed; it has pockets like a rucksack and a collar of red fox fur. I will call him Don Basilio. Whenever I see him he wears an expression of sadness on his face, as if he were listening to a requiem.

Here at the Gare de Lyon he leaped up the steps, his legs making an intense effort but his body hanging back like a rabbit whose stomach is filled with lead. He squeezed through the narrow corridor, pushed the valet aside and, as a crab disappears into sand, backed into his compartment. The Rome Express jerked three times and then moved out of the station.

In the dining car, as the result of an invitation tendered to me by his valet, I found myself seated at Don Basilio's table. It was a profitable arrangement for me, as Don Basilio had brought along his own food and wine, which the steward served, assisted by the valet. We were the object of unpleasant stares from the people being served the ordinary table d'hôte.

After we drank his special brand of Italian coffee, made at the table in a portable machine, he took an immense cigar etui, also of crocodile leather, from a special coat he had changed into, and proffered four Monte Christi. I accepted one and the valet brought forth the kitchen matches with which these cigars are properly lighted. Don Basilio's sad eyes moved from the coffee cup to my face. He leaned back and, with the cigar in his mouth, employed both of his stubby arms to lift one of his short legs over the other. He sighed and, taking the cigar in his right hand and moving the glowing end back and forth under his huge nose, he closed his eyes and said that he wished he were dead. Finally he opened his eyes and asked where I was going.

"To Capri," I said.

"Oh then," he said sadly, "we will be traveling together. Not that we will have any fun. As for me, I have to go there." After a while he added, "I'm Italian—that is, I am of Italian descent—and I have an income of a million lire a day in Italy, but I have to go there to spend it. Can you imagine how stupid that is?" Suddenly he became agitated again, and bowed his head. I glanced around and saw entering an Italian woman of great beauty—a Botticellian kind of Madonna. She wore a blue hat and was severely dressed; she was followed by a distinguished-looking man with a white spade beard. They sat down at one of the tables for four and studied the menu. Don Basilio watched her, his eyes sadder than ever. After a while he said in a muted voice, "How small the world is! Would you believe that over thirty years ago that woman was my love, and that she still is the only one? I knew this trip would be awful—I feel like getting off at the next station.

"Ah, it's terrible to think of it. She is looking intently at the menu but she is not reading it. She is saying to herself, 'So that is Basilio—I knew him when he had black hair and a small waist and was always gay.'" He continued regarding her in one of the many mirrors of the dining car. "Now she is looking up and she is saying to herself, 'And here I sit with you, you dull man.' He is, incidentally, a prince. She is still beautiful, rich and unhappy. I meet her here and there, and always after nodding she looks away and I look away too, because I am responsible for her marriage to that penurious man who has ruined her life. They are going to Capri also; she has a villa there; everybody has a villa in Capri. I know it is going to be awful. You can imagine, now," he said, "with what feelings I approach Capri. I can't stay here any more—it hurts too much to look at her." With these words, he hurried from the car.

Next morning at breakfast, Don Basilio was still thinking of the man with the beard. "He's a snob, and a snob, you know, is out of fashion," said Don Basilio. "When I was a young man in Paris, and richer than anybody else, and the friend of the Prince of Wales, it was fashionable to be a snob. But now who cares a damn who you know and with whom you go?"

The breakfast service was over and most people had left the car. Don Basilio, spurning the menu proffered by the steward, looked with pained mien for his valet.

He went "Psst," and snapped his fingers. "Tell my man to bring us a can of shad roe. I am hungry and it will be about two before we get a decent lunch." The valet came

and set up a large table and we were moved to that. We watched the landscape for a
while, and then ate the shad roe. "I am still very hungry," said Don Basilio. The
servant assured him that a chicken had been put on the fire.

"He doesn't know anything about women—the beard—at any rate, nothing about a
ravishing creature like her," said Don Basilio.

The valet came in and held a dish close to the face of his master, who grunted with
satisfaction. The dining-room steward offered another dish and said, "The asparagus
now?"

"No," said Don Basilio and shook his head. Looking my way, he announced sadly
that he had had a terrible dream.

"You don't want the asparagus with the chicken?" asked the steward.

"No, he doesn't," said the valet.

"Would you like some string beans, signore, or tomatoes, or French-fried potatoes?"
persisted the steward.

"Will you go away?" Don Basilio screamed, and the valet said, "He wants his asparagus after."

"As you like," said the steward, injured, and walked away.

Don Basilio ate the chicken with his fingers and then licked them.

"I dreamt about a wonderful dinner party that I had arranged in Cannes in a beautiful garden—everybody was there. I came a little late and Winston Churchill waved at
me from the terrace. Elsa Maxwell, Lucius Beebe, Obolensky and all the Astors and
Whitneys, and Gilbert Miller and Kitty, and of course the Duke and Duchess of Wind-
sor and the little King and Queen of Yugoslavia were there, and Mona Williams, smiling
with those incredible eyes that are like two star sapphires, and she smiled at me and
waved as I was running up the path. Tallulah Bankhead threw me a kiss, and suddenly
the woman with the blue hat who is on this train smiled at me. But as I was about to
enter the garden Elsa Maxwell ran to the gate and said, 'We're having such a lovely
party—what a pity you weren't asked!' And with this she slammed the gate in my face.
I awoke covered with sweat. I am going to call up my doctor and ask him what such a
dream means. I suppose he will say that insecurity was responsible. Steward! What
time are we getting into Milano?"

"We are a little late—at eleven-twenty, signore."

The station at Milan is one of the monuments to the memory of Mussolini and is
proudly pointed out as such by Italians. It is grandiose and almost of the dimensions
of the Pennsylvania Station in New York. There was a delay sufficient for a tour of the
city.

I changed some money, not very much, but when I wanted to pocket the Italian notes
I got for dollars, it was like trying to put the Sunday edition of the Chicago *Tribune*
into my trouser pocket.

I told a taxi driver that I had a few hours, and asked him to take me to the places of
interest. He stopped briefly at the gas station, on the steel beams above which the bodies

of Mussolini, his mistress and several others had been hung for display. He stopped briefly at the cathedral, and then raced out of the city to the fairgrounds where he offered to show me the most interesting sight in Milan. He parked his cab and led me to a scene both modern and of singular importance in this land. In a hangarlike exhibition hall the products of several competing firms were on view. In back of stout ropes protected by watchmen stood monstrously complicated machines, the size of small houses, making sounds such as come from the interior of establishments in amusement parks that are called "Fun Houses," places where people fall downstairs, get lost in mazes and have air squirted at them.

In this hall, the sounds of joy came from the outside of the fun machine; all other sounds, the hissing and the falling came from the inside. I followed the chauffeur as he pushed his way through the crowd, and I saw that the big machine made spaghetti. Issuing from many openings on the underside of the apparatus a steady endless rain of spaghetti came down onto a conveyor belt and was thus transported to another machine, operated by attendants in white suits and gloves. The spaghetti, the driver pointed out, was real, and that was very important, because close to the machine, which was of Italian make, was one made by a Swiss firm, and nobody looked at this, although it appeared even more modern and elegant. It was running, but made no noise, and the frugal Swiss had substituted artificial spaghetti made of nylon—in which no Italian had any interest.

I had to pull the driver away from the exhibition. He pointed at other machines and told me that those manufactured macaroni, ravioli and so forth. The train for Rome was made up when we got back.

Don Basilio and his valet were in a rage because the accommodations they had engaged were not in order. I had been alone in a compartment from Paris to Milan. But now I found myself in another sleeping car and sharing my compartment with another passenger. He came aboard with an Italian girl, and both of them inspected the compartment carefully. He walked out into the corridor with the girl and, as the departure of the train was announced, he enacted a farewell scene with her that was ardent even here. He then ran to the compartment, pushed up the window and threw kisses at her as the train got under way. Finally, he took a large handkerchief from his sleeve and waved it.

Until he spoke to me in English and said he was a Londoner he had seemed French or Italian; he was dressed in a polyglot costume of yellow corduroy jacket, gray flannel slacks, neglected gray suede shoes and a Borsalino hat; he carried a cane and had a raincoat over his arm, and the suitcase he put on the bed was old and worn. Like Don Basilio, he was heavy, a man weighing a little less than Alfred Hitchcock. He had taken possession of the lower berth as a matter of course. No one could expect of him the gymnastics with which he would have gained the upper.

After dinner some hours out of Milan, and after a great deal of attention to getting ready for bed, he turned out the light. He seemed nervous, he kept turning and moving,

and the noise of his bed was added to the rattling of the train on the worn-out roadbed.
Later he got up, raised the window shade, stared briefly out into the night, and then
went to bed again. I let him know that I was awake and he excused himself, saying,
"In a moment she will come." I became a little worried and asked him who would come.

"My bridge," he said excitedly, adding, "in a little while the train will slow down."

I thought that perhaps he wanted to jump off the bridge. I remembered his passionate farewell at the station and for the next few seconds I debated whether I should try to stop him, pull the emergency cord or let him jump.

"Here she comes," he said in high treble. He pushed up the window and leaned out. As the first girder of the bridge slowly took shape in the dim light cast by the train window, he reached out, touched it tenderly, and said, "Hello, old girl." I felt better when at last he pulled his head back into the car and said to me, "You know, I built this bridge during the war."

He leaned out again and watched until the whole train had crossed the bridge.

As the train resumed speed there was a commotion in the corridor. It involved an American girl, an Italian youth, the conductor and a middle-aged businessman from Chicago. The girl, it developed, had met the young man in Milan while they were staying at the same hotel. They had met again in the restaurant car and had had a few drinks. Later, as she was about to retire, she found the young man in the same sleeping compartment with her. She promptly called the conductor, who listened drowsily while the young man explained that he had arranged the sleeping accommodations with the *portier* of the Milan hotel where he and the girl had stayed, and that it was customary here to share train compartments with friends or even strangers of the opposite sex. The conductor seconded the young man and said that it was quite all right, and that no one thought anything about it. The man from Chicago, who, it seemed, had also been in the restaurant car, came up during the argument. He listened a while, standing up with difficulty. Then, leaning heavily on the conductor, he offered his protection to the young girl.

She was bewildered until he explained that he was a father and a very important man, that he had a whole compartment to himself, and that he would put the young man with the ideas into the vacant bed of his own room. The young man quickly retired into his compartment and locked the door, and the girl went back to the restaurant car.

The protector now awoke everybody with a loud tirade on the moral concepts of Europe and of Italy in particular. The object of his lecture was the pale conductor who had been sleeping when the disturbance started. Conductors in European sleeping cars fold up on a seat at the end of the corridor and cover themselves with a blanket.

The father from Chicago staggered up and down the car and began pounding on compartment doors. No one got mad at him; eventually the apathy in the sleeping car wearied him and he went to bed, and the normal night noises of the train took over.

I came into the dining car very late the next morning and found Don Basilio almost through breakfast. He looked even more like a wax figure in the morning light. He lifted his nose and sniffed. "Spaghetti," he said.

"Yes," said the steward, "we are eating now, back there—the cooks and the stewards."

"I'd very much like some of your spaghetti," said Don Basilio, "enough for me and 31
my friend here." The steward was delighted.

The spaghetti came, cooked with butter and garlic and with a handful of chopped
parsley strewn over it.

"Some people condemn the Italian kitchen," said Don Basilio, "and also the French.
They say that they can't eat the food on account of the garlic. Now there is no good
cooking except with garlic—but in the hands of a bad cook it's poisonous. It must be
used with extreme care. The most reckless are the English; once they take to garlic
cooking they use it so freely that it is impossible even for an Italian to eat it. For
example, in Aix-en-Provence—a city where they overdo garlic—once I was served
truffles wrapped in bacon, a very good dish. The truffles profit by the flavor of the
bacon, the bacon is enhanced by the truffles, and I like it. But at that luncheon I bit into
a truffle and inside was a whole clove of garlic. Both the truffle and bacon were ruined.
And the garlic, which, incidentally, was also in the chicken we were served and on
the toast that came with the cheese and in the salad—it was so predominant that
the whole meal was ruined. Now take this spaghetti—simple, ultrasimple—but with
a bouquet like the finest wine."

The train stopped at a small station to wait for a clear track. Outside the window
were the cars of a freight train. The boxcar doors were open, and inside were benches
on which sat people most of whom had no shoes, and all of whose eyes were fixed on the
spaghetti and the bottle of wine on our table. I said that it seemed to me that in Italy
there was a belief that God had made some people rich and others poor and that the
tragedy was that not only the rich but the poor, also, believed it, and that in consequence, it would never change.

Don Basilio answered: "And don't you think that is as it should be and is a very good
arrangement? Have you ever seen an Italian peasant envious of those who have fine
cars, or horses, or jewels? No, they admire those things, knowing that they never can
have them for themselves. They adopt a detachment, like people who go to the theater
or to an art gallery, admiring priceless paintings, glad to know that they exist, but also
knowing that they never could own them. Just looking at these things, they derive a
pleasure that possession never brings, because possession means worry." He snapped
his finger. "More," he shouted back to the table of the steward.

"You are going where?" he asked with the coffee.

"To Capri," I said.

"Oh yes, you told me. I will see you on the train to Naples," he said and added that
he would take a short sleep and then look after his baggage himself. "I have asked
the Italian ambassador in Paris if he could guarantee there would be no revolution
for the next six months, and he promised there would be none. But then, Italians
promise you anything. Incidentally, you have picked the worst season to come to
Capri." With these final observations, and after handing the steward a royal tip, he
left the car.

There was an overnight stop in Rome. In the grill of the Hotel Excelsior, which is the equal of the Stork Club's Cub Room in New York, he sat down with me.

"She is upstairs," he said, "the woman with the blue hat." He had a great capacity for wine, and I returned his hospitality with three quarts of Bollinger. Sunk in a Gargantuan leather *fauteuil* at four in the morning, with a few of the better street-walkers of Rome hanging on the bar, and dabbing at his eyes, Don Basilio told the story of the woman with the blue hat.

"How is it," he began, "that one never finds it a second time—you know, the ideal love? I mean the kind of love for which the head, the heart and the body are all in accord. I had the loveliest parents anyone could ask for. I was the only child and they gave me everything. Maybe that is what is wrong with me—until recently I had everything, and yet never was I truly happy. But I was talking about my lovely parents. They said good morning to each other with smiling faces, and they held each other by the hand for a long while several times a day. They loved each other so beautifully, and as only Italians can love. They sang together, that is, Mamma played the piano and Papa sang opera in Italian and French, and songs by Schubert, and there was peace and happiness in their hearts and in our home—they never needed to go out. Each night before they went to sleep they sat in their bed and folded their hands and prayed aloud together like children. We lived then in Brazil and once a year came to Italy. On these trips we always went to Capri, and it was so beautiful then, because *she* was there—the woman in the blue hat.

"I long so for companionship like this, for the great love, but I can't find it because it comes to you only once, and if you are dumb and spoiled as I was, you let it go— you don't recognize it. Let me tell you how I threw away the only love I have ever had from a good girl. She was from one of the finest families; she was that combination of happy and serious girl that you find only in Italy—elegant, kind, beautiful and proud. My parents found her altogether to their liking and blessed her as their own. I was eighteen, she was sixteen and all was prepared for marriage. In nothing was there a flaw. We were both religious in the same degree, not too much, not too little; we liked the same things, and we did not have to speak, for we were happy just walking along hand in hand—oh, how lightly we walked—as on clouds. It was the perfect love.

"She came to me one day with six little leather books all carefully bound, and she said, 'Basilio, since I will be your wife, you must know all about me, about every hour's happening. Here in these books is the story of my life so far, all I have thought and done. Take them and read them.' I took them. I must say I was frankly bored by what was in them—silly things, romantic nonsense, the life of a little girl; church, games, excursions, school, about a little new brother, about a new dress, all stuff like that. I don't know why I bothered to read them in order—perhaps because I was so very much in love with her, and when she was not there in person, she was there in the book. I had no thoughts but of her. So, in book No. 4, I came to a passage that said: 'Went to a concert with Mariano.' He was a boy I could never stand. It went on, 'And we sat in the park on a stone bench and he was nice, he did not speak fresh with me, he did not try to kiss me or put his arm around me, or even hold my hand. He sat there and I felt that he was very glad I was with him, and I changed my mind about him and promised that from now on I would be nicer to him and treat him like a brother. On the way home I took his arm.' That was all there was in the book—or in any of them—about Mariano. But the next page was empty. The only empty page in all the little books—do you know, on account of that empty page, I did not marry that girl. Crazy fool that I am, I was jealous of that empty page. I ruined my chance for happiness and hers—that's why I look away when I see her."

His hands, tightly clasped all during the story, relaxed.

"Nothing does me any good any more," he said. The streetwalkers sat along the bar like vultures, waiting. "But the heart doesn't stop aching." He started worrying about his baggage. "I'll have to see to the packing," he said and got up.

The elevators in the Excelsior are like quick little taxis, they fly up with zest. "From now on," said Don Basilio, "it will be awful. Here you must take care of all things yourself," he said, "lock every bag, lock every door, keep your hands in your pockets."

He, speaking Italian, would be all right, he said. But of all foreigners—and especially Americans—beggars, porters and other natives who come in contact with them have two opinions: first, that they are all millionaires; second, that all of them are idiots.

Don Basilio offered to take care of my luggage, but I had my trunk checked through to Capri.

"I hope you find it there," he said mournfully.

I have one small bag which I always carry myself. The article that usually takes up most room in this bag is a book that has been at my elbow for years. It weighs three pounds and its pages have narrow margins; it is set in extremely small type and was printed in the years 1856 to 1877, by F. A. Brockhaus, in Leipzig. I recommend the volume to anyone who can read German. The title is *Wanderjahre in Italien* (Wander Years in Italy), and the name of the author is Ferdinand Gregorovius. I took the volume out of the bag the next day aboard the train. It was toward evening, midway between Rome and Naples. The landscape outside was on page 213 of the book:

> Who is able to paint it, this magnificent terrain, at the hour when all the hills glow in the purple play of evening and when the valleys below them sink into shadow? The night slides upward on the hills, its hand reaches up to the cities that stand on top of them, for one after the other until all are taken in darkness.
>
> In the windows of the highest and most distant still glitters the sinking sun in pale red rays—there in Seronne, in Rojate—and now only in Piglio—and now that last flicker is extinguished also.
>
> I ride my horse here on this road—the impression of a great landscape is heightened for the thinking man, when he knows how to rhyme it with history, for it is thereby animated.

This road, this strip of land beneath our feet, is the key to the Kingdom of Naples, it is the strategic highway of the people of the Middle Ages.

Of the Goths, the Vandals, the Franks, the Longobards, of Delizar, or the Ottones—even of Saracens, Frenchmen and Spaniards—of uncounted people whose horses drank from the waters of the river Sacco.

The serene landscape now was in complete darkness, the electric train was rapid, and we had eaten aboard simply but well. Don Basilio, opposite me, had closed his eyes.

In my mind unknown places always have a very definite character, color and shape, determined by hearsay, instinct and reading. I imagined Capri a sugar-loaf-shaped mountain that rose out of lukewarm water. It was dark brown. On its rotund plateau was a city made up of luxurious hotels, bars, villas and casinos. They were crowded at the proper season with the nomads from Palm Beach, Cannes and St. Moritz. I expected to behold a shining tabernacle of ennui.

The steward tried to make conversation with Don Basilio, saying something about the state of the world. Don Basilio snapped: "I don't worry about the state of the world at all, you know—all I care about is to give some pleasure to my friends. Bring us another bottle of wine." The steward hastened away and Don Basilio said, "Did you see it? It's as it was in France. The steward is walking about in canvas sneakers and one has a hole cut in it for the bunion. It was like that in my club when I came back first. It gives me pain to look at anything like that. There are in this life moments when one does not want to belong to the human race. Well . . . I am losing my appetite for living all over again." I had Gregorovius opened at the chapter on Capri.

I closed the book, the train slowed down and the lights of the first houses of Naples moved into the windows.

A few minutes later we stood on the platform and the valet handed the baggage out to several youths, one of whom, in charge of the band, was arguing with Don Basilio, who refused to pay what he demanded. In Rome, he said, there were uniformed porters and they had been honest, but here it was sinister.

"*Bandidos*," he called them, and the money that he offered was refused. Either two thousand lire to deliver the luggage or nothing, the boy said. He finally got almost what he asked for.

The bargain was closed through the mediation of a friend of Don Basilio's who had come to meet him. The *bandidos* stacked the exquisite luggage into a small cart and, with several of them hauling it, disappeared into the night.

"I'll never see my luggage again," said Don Basilio.

The Excelsior Hotel in Naples is one of the cleanest I have ever seen, its rooms are immense, the corridors slippery with polish and on the tiled floor of the bar is a replica of the Bay of Naples. The alcoholic father from Chicago was sitting there, glass in hand, studying the territory around Vesuvio and Portici. I took the elevator up to

look at the view from the window of my room. The Bay of Naples lay in moonlight. Over on the crater of Vesuvio rested a crescent-shaped cloud; the lights of Sorrento and those of Ischia and Capri were flickering, and, in the sea, like stars reflected from overhead, danced the lights of fishing boats. A tenor in an open-air restaurant below sang the worn-out melody of "Santa Lucia." It was like a souvenir postcard, but also, as most such places are, startling rather than beautiful until you become familiar with them. The eye takes inventory, the contours are traced on the mind, you drink it up. Slowly it becomes yours, and the postcard vanishes; the scene's magnificence puts you in bondage. I pulled a chair to the window and sat awed by the scene for several hours. It's a good thing to look upon it, the first time, in the night.

The next morning I took a hansom cab from the hotel to the pier.

Adjacent to a square as tumultuous as the floor of the New York Stock Exchange, and in which everyone is half naked, is a pier at which lie little boats that go to Ischia, Posillipo and Amalfi.

From here also leaves a small motor ship named *Capri.* The fare is about fifty cents. The boat is something like a ferry. The seats are hard, and below deck is a bar. It was a hot day. Don Basilio and his servant arrived late, and all the seats were taken. The baggage problem was easy now.

"I knew it—I told you it was risky—they stole my baggage, all of it. I had to run out and buy shirts and shoes today—and it's no use to complain to the police," he said loudly, and the people around him nodded as he mopped his face.

"Listen to what happened here," said one. "A man had a new car, an American of course, and a boy came up to his car and spat in his face. The American stopped the car and got out to run after the boy, and another boy got in and drove off with the new car. He never saw it again."

Don Basilio turned to the rest of the passengers and told them again about his luggage. They nodded with sympathy and agreed that something had to be done.

"Ah," Don Basilio said to me, "the crooks that stole my luggage are perhaps here among us, nodding also, and looking for what else they can pick off me."

The ship rolled as soon as it left the breakwater, and when it was abreast of Sorrento half the people were seasick. The roll changed to pitching as the ship came into the narrow channel between the mainland and Capri, although there was hardly any sea.

Jean Paul Richter compares the shape of Capri to a Sphinx. Gregorovius said of it: "It's like an ancient sarcophagus whose sides are adorned with snaky-haired furies." It has been compared to a boot and to a crocodile. I did not find it to be similar to anything. It is as definite in shape as a table, a crocodile or the Sphinx, but it has its own shape and compels your attention. You feel it to be as ancient as the sea, you look at it with the curiosity with which you would study the face of an interesting and perhaps disturbed person. It is altogether different from the picture that I had in mind.

The ship passed into calm water. At the entrance of the harbor, Don Basilio was telling a fellow South American in Portuguese about his baggage. Next to me sat a man and a woman, American tourists. The man had almost been seasick several times and now, as the ship became steady, he talked to the woman next to him, resuming a conversation interrupted by his distress.

"Well, forty bucks a week was a lot of money and so I was a reporter for a while, and then that columnist wanted an assistant, and I went over there and after a couple of years the columnist dies. Oh, you know, nothing nasty—no keyhole stuff or scandal, just a kind of mellow column, like Sobol writes, reminiscing stuff, faces along the avenue, stuff like that, and I was in—I was making three hundred bucks a week and the struggle was over. It's no use marrying unless you do it right and go the whole way. Well, we moved out to this community and I said I didn't want to live there if they wouldn't accept us—I didn't want to have anything to do with them, in fact.

"Well, across the street from us was a house where they entertained a lot. Once they had the Earl of Derby or somebody like that—that kind of people, you know. Well, they asked us to the next party, forty people, that's twenty couples, and ever since then we've just been as welcome as that first time. All I can say, it's a lovely place and they're as nice folks as you find. I'll tell you about a typical weekend. We get together, a gang, you know, about eight highly select couples, and we start out

with a cocktail at the Ogdens', and then we go to a Saturday-night dinner dance at   37
the country club—you know what that's like, it's pleasant living. It's really nice—a
big buffet and nice people having a fine time. Well, that's where I'd like to be right
now—I'll go along that far. But Clarabel—she's not satisfied with that, she's got to
travel. She's got to follow them over here—and they own a villa—naturally, it's on
Capri. And we've been invited to stay as long as we like. Well, I don't like it a bit.
In fact, I don't care a damn about all this stuff. Now that man over there had all his
luggage stolen yesterday and—Lord!—the food."

The engines were signaled to stop and the columnist got up to look for his wife.
She lay on a bench, and the pleasant baby face that she must have worn at other times
was old, and the utter misery of seasickness was in her eyes. With a weak smile she
thanked a little unshaven padre for recovering a little ruined hat that had blown off
her head. The columnist took the hat and the padre, in his other hand, held out a
small box bearing a picture of St. Francis of Assisi. The columnist looked at his wife,
saw that she had closed her eyes again, and put a folded bill in the poor box. Then he
said, "Hey, Clarabel, here's Capri."

The ship was now turning to back up against the pier, and on the pier sat the
bandido of the night before, with all the luggage of Don Basilio.

ISLE OF CAPRI

CAPRI

HERE IS a simple recipe for understanding the conformation of the island of Capri: place on the table before you, to the left, an ordinary coffee cup turned upside down; to its right place an oversized coffee cup, also inverted, and preferably with a chipped lip, toward you. Put a matchbox between the two cups, move the three objects close together and drape a pale green handkerchief over the lot—and that is roughly Capri. You're looking at it now as you approach it from the north—from Naples. The small cup is Mount Tiberio (1096 feet), the large cup is Mount Solaro (1920 feet), and in the valley between, atop the matchbox, is the town of Capri. Rest a match end up on the table, leaning against the box, and now you have the funicular that takes you down to the Marina Grande, the large port; at approximately the same spot on the other side of the island is the Marina Piccola, the small port without benefit of funicular. On that side you can drape two limp strands of spaghetti to simulate the roads that lead from Capri down to the water. Loop one piece in generous serpentine turns—that's the one traveled by buses. Arrange the other in tight zigzags; it is the Via Krupp, a gift of the late munitions manufacturer. If you can expend two more pieces of spaghetti—a long one from Capri up to Anacapri, on the big cup, and another down to the Marina Grande, you will have just about all the roads. A path leads to the top of the small cup, where the ruins of the magnificent Villa Jove are located. Like the houses of the great in Pompeii, it was most restrained and simple. By comparison, for example, with Versailles, or with Mr. Hearst's palatial San Simeon in California, it was merely a weekend bungalow. The fine pagan mood of this great ruin is marred by a badly sculptured modern Madonna, planted in the middle of it so that you seldom escape the clash of mediocre ecclesiastic art with the purity of the classic.

Such clashes offend you again and again in Italy, and this is difficult to explain. For, with all the great models in front of them, and the blood of the best painters and sculptors in their veins, the Italians recently have produced very little in the way of good art.

There is the Blue Grotto, represented by the chipped place on the big cup; it also is decorated with an abominably executed Madonna that occupies a niche over the entrance. The roof of this tunnel is so low that you enter it sitting on the bottom of a small rowboat; even so, you have to duck while the boatman takes you in by pulling on a chain. The Blue Grotto is all that you have heard of it. The renditions of it that one finds on cheap souvenir paintings all over Capri come closest to the truth, and particularly accurate is the light effect on the top and the sidewalls. The local artists treat it as if they were showing a cavern with luminous, bluish worms crawling up the walls and across the vaulted ceiling.

On top of the smaller of the two coffee cups, on a rocky promontory that rises above Capri, is a villa with a sweeping view of the Mediterranean on both sides of the island. It is owned by Prince Gaetano Parente, who has the long legs to negotiate several times a day the two-hundred-odd stone steps by which the villa is reached.

He is never without a small dog, a breed peculiar to the island and, like its population, of the most varied nomenclature.

"Without inflicting on you the tyranny of dates and too many names," said Gaetano Parente, "I will give you the briefest kind of history of Capri." We were walking down the Via Krupp. That is, he was walking—I ran.

"Almost everyone who has written a book here has taken something from a volume called *Ricerche Storiche sull' Isola di Capri,* by Rosario Mangoni. I recommend it to you, and also one called *The Book of Capri,* by Harold E. Trower, onetime British consul here. One cannot write about Italy without quoting from one book or another, or from inscriptions on ancient metals, stones, wood, canvases or tapestries that are in evidence everywhere.

"The story goes something like this: the Emperor Augustus saw Capri's possibilities, and it was he, not Tiberius, who built it up. Tiberius came later and improved it, making of it for a while a rest place and camp for soldiers of the Roman Empire. His name is more in evidence here today than that of Augustus.

"After Tiberius, Capri for a few hundred years was left to solitude. I'll spare you history here and we will move up to when it was rediscovered as a pleasure place, by Germans, of all people, who at the time headed a spiritual back-to-nature movement. They came here, shouted '*Wunderbar,*' and walked about naked carrying their children on both shoulders. They lived on fruits and vegetables, picked wildflowers and named butterflies that until then had never been properly catalogued.

"After these blond nudists, the English arrived—the Oxford boys, the Shelley and Keats group, and they were very impressed by the fine physiques of the native fishermen. Those romantic boys did a lot for Capri, constantly singing its praises. They never tired of adoring this happy, brown people and, strangely enough, the propaganda brought on a great horde of British spinsters. There was no harbor then, and the good ladies were carried ashore in the strong arms of the picturesque natives. Then came other English breeds, noblemen, industrialists and archeologists who bought the best statuary and shipped it to the British Museum.

"Now Capri was really famous. The kings came and the Russian grand dukes; the Kaiser visited on his yacht. All the world came—the old rich, the *nouveaux riches,* and tycoons like Krupp and Axel Wenner-Gren; also Stalin, and even Trotsky. Now an American woman, Mrs. Harrison Williams, is the Queen of the Isle. Of Italians, we have relatively few.

"Of all the things that have gone on here you find the remnants not only in the earth but also in the faces about you. Giovanni is a fisherman at the Marina Grande— his face is out of the senate chambers of Rome in the time of Augustus. Put a toga on the fat chauffeur that drives the Anacapri bus, and you have Nero. Look at the man coming out of the Restaurant Hidigeigei every day after lunch; he wears his beard like Franz Josef of Hapsburg and looks like him. It's all preserved here as in an album, including some of the English who still adore the native fishermen. The English spinsters now are fewer on account of travel restrictions, but then we have the Americans who outdo everyone else in letting their hair down and admiring everything, especially a few American women who admire the fishermen even more violently than do the English boys . . ."

With that much history we had arrived at a restaurant where, in a neat little kitchen, a simple and very reasonable meal was prepared. The curious regulations of the island forbid the sale of wine here, and in consequence it's the one place where one can't have spaghetti. To serve spaghetti one must serve wine, and this, constituting a proper Italian restaurant, demands a restaurant license. The woman who runs the little inn has never been able to afford the license, and so the place is called a tearoom. This small establishment, named the Pension Weber, is at Marina Piccola and overlooks a beach and rows of little bathhouses. The son of the proprietress waited on table, but he was not too gay, having been called up from the beach to help out.

A sunburned man with the small gold medal of the Madonna hanging from his neck was telling a woman who sat at his table that he had come to Capri to look around for a villa.

Gaetano Parente said to me, "Here is the most important thing to know about Capri: never say to anybody that you want to buy a villa. I will tell you all about villas. There are three main real estate agents here. One is an old duke who is a communist; another is an old Russian princess who was, some sixty-five years ago, very beautiful—one can see that even now, but one cannot understand a single word she says. Then there is a German baroness, also a beauty of long ago. This last one, being German, is of course methodical and knows what she wants and she occasionally sells a villa—the others only go through the motions.

"Everybody else, from the priest of the biggest church in Capri to the last fisherman on the Punta Tragara and also the gatekeeper of the ruins of the Villa Jove, is a real estate agent. Each is a poet, and mostly they sell places that exist only in their imaginations. Of course, most people who ask about villas don't want to buy them anyway, so it's just a Capri pastime.

"Let us assume you really decide to buy something—almost everything is for sale. You find the villa you like, knock on the door and ask the owner what he wants for it. The owner says, 'I want ten million lire.' Not being an Italian, you say 'Good,' and you go to the bank and come back with the money. Now he says, 'Ah, my wife (or my cousin, or my father), who owns half of this house, will not sell for this price.' 'Good,' you say—'How much then?' 'Twelve million,' he says. You bring the additional two million. Now he remembers that a grandchild, of whom he is the guardian, has an interest, and he cannot cheat the little one—he did not think about this before. 'Let's make it fifteen million and not talk any more,' he says.

"Now you go and bring the rest of the money and you think that finally the villa, at fifteen million lire, is yours.

"But there are other things—a relative who is a lawyer appears, and he speaks about a small commission due him. Then he tells you that the garden has to be bought and—another thing overlooked—in the attic lives the grandmother of the owner. She's so good and sweet, and she goes with the villa; you can of course make some other arrangements for her. Also, this lawyer draws you into a corner and whispers to you that you can't possibly want this peasant hut to live in. 'I will show you a villa,' he mutters, and describes a place like the Alhambra. By the time you have it, the usual villa comes to between ten and fifteen million lire (or up to about $26,000). Now I will tell you of the servants, but that part is pure joy.

"The servants are the best part of the villa. Born with shrewdness and skill as are all Italians, they don't speak Italian at all, but a Neapolitan dialect. Yet they manage to understand English, French, German, Czech or Swedish; other languages, like Hindustani or Arabic, they understand by merely looking intently at the speaker and reading his mind. They are very clean and they give you every comfort; they live only for you. They want to satisfy every one of your wishes. If one night you come home a little unsteady and gay and ask them for the moon, they will bring it to you, or else they will improvise something that is as good.

"The first party you give at your villa is very important to them; they watch everything closely. They want to see how you pour whiskey, how fast the bottles of champagne are opened, what kind of flowers you order for your house, what tips you give to messengers, what orders you issue for food. From all this they determine exactly how much to steal. They do this so nicely that you don't mind it at all. The salaries they get are ridiculous, but of no great importance—what makes them happy is to cheat a little on the macaroni, to move a bottle of wine from your side of the cellar to theirs.

"I forgot to tell you that among villas here you have the most extraordinary assortment to choose from. This isle has always attracted remarkable people, and so you may find yourself owning a place completely Chinese, including the opium pipes with which the last owner smoked himself to death. Or you may find a small castle with stone bulwarks and cannons; you may become the owner of a house whose builder was devoted to Mayan culture, tiger hunting, deep-sea fishing or the collection of ancient timepieces. If your house lacks decoration, take a shovel and dig in your garden. I came up with the jaw of a prehistoric animal and a bas-relief the first day. Now I have decorated one whole wall of my studio with the things I dug up. Some are so very interesting—well, I cannot show them to everyone."

I was most grateful to Prince Gaetano Parente. Actually, I didn't want to buy a villa, but I rented one. Its name was lettered on a piece of tile at the gate, together with a picture of the owner. It was something like La Balalaika. The house was nice, but the name didn't go with either the place or the island, and I couldn't remember it, so I changed it to Jovina, meaning the Little Villa Jove.

I have a preference for irregularity in houses and Jovina was just right. It stood

48 hidden by olive trees extending halfway down to the sea and was bordered by little vineyards and an immense terrace which afforded a wonderful view. At the right of it rose the wall of Mount Solaro, beyond the top of which the sun passed at about four o'clock, leaving the terrace in pleasant shade for the rest of the day. The view included the Faraglioni—three rocks that jut out of the water off Punta Tragara—the Marina Piccola and the sea. Best of all, the place was completely lost, yet only a few minutes' shaded walk from the town of Capri. The rent was a hundred dollars a month, plus the food for four cats.

"How about the cats?" I said to the landlady on taking over.

"The cats go with the villa," she said, "and also Antonia."

Antonia was seventeen; she arrived at seven in the morning, left at 9 P.M. and got a salary of three dollars a month. Her first job was to pump water from the cistern below the villa up into a tank on the roof. This she did for three quarters of an hour every morning, singing in Neapolitan.

Lithe and quick as the salamanders in the garden, she leaped to a boulder and up on the roof several times during the pumping to check the amount of water, always smiling. Next she lit the charcoal oven and with a small fan got the fire going. She was transported when her salary was trebled and her hours cut in half. My guests were her guests—whatever concerned me became her worry or joy.

One morning I climbed up on the roof with an empty bottle and a long piece of string. I tied one end of the string around the bottle, which I floated in the water tank. Then I lowered the other end of the string, with a mule shoe tied to it, down the side of the house. Next, I marked a scale on the wall, so that Antonia could read the water level in the tank without jumping up on the roof. This invention raised her esteem to delirium, and all the water girls of the neighborhood were called. They came running barefoot and, shy as doves, appeared from the shadows of the olive trees. "He, my signore, did it," said Antonia, pointing with pride at me and at the indicator of our water tank.

Whenever she saw me anywhere in Capri, she would run to me and walk by my side a while; or if she were in a hurry, she'd wave. She was always neat and, in addition, she had humor. My mother came to visit me and, upon realizing the utter remoteness of the place, she said, "My God, don't leave me alone in this house at night—somebody could easily murder me." Therefore on one occasion I said to Antonia, "Will you sleep here tonight?" and she said, "Yes, signore, but I think I better ask my mamma." So I said, "Tell her that my mamma is afraid at night, and that I am going out tonight and that's why I want you to stay with her."

She smiled—and said sweetly, "Oh, for that—I don't have to ask."

A family renting a villa like Jovina, shopping in the markets and doing its own cooking, can live well now in Capri on not much more than a hundred dollars a month.

I know a couple of Swedes with healthy appetites who lived in comfort in Anacapri for seventy-five dollars a month.

When I took over the Villa Jovina, the landlady presented me with a twenty-page inventory which carefully listed every broken cup and saucer, a broom that looked like an abused polo mallet and even a dishrag. A lawyer came on her behalf. Everything was checked over when I moved in and again when I departed. And in the meantime the landlady herself lived in a grotto under the house. She emerged early every morning and went down to the gate where, with a wild yell and a rending sound such as is heard when a doctor rips adhesive tape from a wrenched shoulder, she tore off the sign *Villa Jovina*. Right after breakfast—and without a word from me—Antonia always brought me a new piece of cardboard, India ink and brush and, standing by, she watched me paint the day's new sign. She held it in the sun to dry and then, running down the stairs, singing all the while, she attached it to the tile with new strips of adhesive tape. I painted the sign sixty times in all, staying there that many days. The four cats were fat when I left in spite of the eleven members of Antonia's family, who got half the meat and fish bought for the cats. There was also a little graft with the iceman. Otherwise, Antonia was scrupulously honest.

The Piazza, the center of the social life of Capri, is a stage on which movement, sound and lighting seem to be manipulated by a director of untiring invention. The audience sits on the set; the set is on many levels. There is a complicated and interesting white church, reminiscent of the Cathedral in Quito, Ecuador. It is the only church I have ever seen in the basement of which is a bar and café. There are vaulted exits and entrances to the Piazza, and an open break at one side offers the cyclorama of the Bay of Naples. There, forming one side of that opening, stands a square clock tower with a set of bells that bongs every few minutes with such insistence that the glasses on the tables begin to dance and tinkle and people cover their ears. At the base of the tower is a police station the size of a telephone booth, and a newsstand where you can buy American magazines and comic books, the latter translated into Italian. Superman here is called *La Battaglia di Orson*. At about noon you can also see Orson Welles walking across the Piazza.

The center of the Piazza is crammed with the varicolored sidewalk tables of four competing restaurants and the tight-fitting, shapeless wicker chairs that belong to them. The greatest activity in the Piazza is toward seven in the evening.

There are many people in Capri who, in less romantic and non-Italian regions, would find themselves in strait jackets and not permitted to walk about without attendants close by. There are among this group several outstanding and amusing ones. One little man, a retired civil servant from Naples, has a suit with electric bulbs for buttons connected to a battery in his coat pocket. On high holidays he stands in the center of the Piazza where from time to time and with great seriousness he lights himself up. There is a poet who lives at the Marina Piccola and writes an ode on the soles of his shoes every morning. Then, walking up to the Piazza, he eradicates the daily inspiration in the sand of the road.

During one busy hour, a native not given to bragging pointed out to me forty-six male homosexuals sitting in the Piazza. The crowd totaled perhaps a thousand people, and though this percentage seems high, I think it is equaled if not surpassed in other fashionable places over the world. The majority of them are respectable people, and unless you are especially allergic, they provide you with the stock comedy drama they perform everywhere. Their female counterparts are here in about the same number.

Toward nine, various members of the sleeping-pill set and the narcotic squad march in. They are of mixed nationality and include several Americans. They are starry-eyed and dressed as for an elegant masquerade, the men in black or wine-colored velvet slacks, golden sandals, rings the size of matchboxes and lavalieres hanging on bronzed chests. The women are exquisitely gowned. I heard much talk of their orgies, and attended several of them. Whatever happened there that was awful must have taken place inside their heads, for I never saw any of them behave badly. One of them had the face of a saint in perpetual ecstasy; many of them appeared to float past me and disappear. They remained alert all through the night and seemed to enjoy especially the early morning hours. Since they were all extremely young, there was as yet no evidence of punishment in their faces. Next day they were as radiant in the sea as on the ballroom floor.

The natives who labor pass through the Piazza constantly. Mostly they are like a troupe of acrobats accompanying their equipment into a circus ring. Silently, on bare feet or straw-soled canvas shoes, they move along with dignity and grace. Two pull a small wagon while two walk behind with ropes with which to hold back the wagon on the sharp declines of the narrow streets. They are as alert as the addicts, and most of them are as gay. They slow down in the Piazza, crying politely, "*Permesso,*" asking people to let them pass, and as they pass, they inspect the crowd with curiosity. Children and women in tattered clothes, carrying great loads on their heads, and men bearing produce and baggage, stones, sand and timber in astonishing weights cross through the Piazza, for no automobile or horse-and-wagon can go beyond the Piazza. They sometimes stop to rest there, without removing their burdens. They stand and gaze at the crowds, astonished at first, like people looking at strange animals in the zoo. I have studied their faces, and in none of them have I observed envy or resentment; if anything, besides the expression of awe, there is a look of pity.

Add to the foregoing groups and individuals a dozen priests, a few professional invalids walking and standing about, half a dozen fishermen, six Frenchmen at a table for two, a group from Hollywood—and some people from the ringside of El Morocco; include in the late hours a few rich American women with their hangers-on, a handful of international panderers and here and there an honest-to-God tourist and his wife, and the picture of the Piazza is complete. At the height of the season, when every hotel room is taken, old cars no longer in running order are dragged here, and people pay to sit in them, or even sleep all night in them.

Under the platform on which stand the small green bathing cabins at the Marina Piccola are a few white-painted boats which are called *sandolinis*. This boat has the shape of a sardine as it is seen from above, and one balances on it like riding a bicycle over a tightwire with the hands off the bars. The *sandolini* is nine feet in length; midship is a square recess like a well, or cockpit, and in this sits the rider, propelling himself with

a double-ended paddle. Once you know how to use the *sandolini* you can move along at a good speed.

I hired one of these every day and rowed to a rock from which I swam. In a week I became proficient enough to ride as the natives do—that is, sitting up on the small deck with the feet in the well. After two weeks of this, on a day when the sea seemed calm, I started at the Marina Piccola and, paddling past my rock and on westward beyond the Grotto Verde, I steered for the lighthouse at Punta Carena. In another two hours of steady and not tiring paddling I went by the Blue Grotto and came to the Baths of Tiberio, where I swam and ate. I went on after an hour's rest and paddled to the Marina Grande, and then set out to finish circumnavigating the island by skirting the massive cliff (the small coffee cup) on the top of which is the Castle of Tiberio. A boat passed me, and the people waved. Going around the east end of the island I came into the strait between Sorrento and Capri, and the color of the water changed from green to slate; and in the channel, suddenly, were whitecaps. I kept close to the rocks and paddled. The sea lifted me up about ten feet and after every rise, in a sickening cork-screw motion, the *sandolini* sank down—or rather was sucked down and against the rocky bottom. It was too late to turn around, and it would have been too difficult to paddle against the wind back to the Marina Grande. I will always remember the stern of the boat from which people had waved, as it disappeared behind the mountain.

Along this coast are many grottoes, and from them come noises made by the action of the sea. Some of these sounds are as if a herd of thirsty beasts were drinking, while others roar; some, as a wave rises, make a hissing sound and shoot out a jet of compressed air mixed with water. There are grottoes that moan awfully—and sigh. I came to one that gave the illusion of the doors of a vast bank vault being shut; every fearful noise of watery catastrophe was along this passage. I managed by rowing fast to keep the *sandolini* atop some waves like a surfboat. Looking up I saw the rock from which Tiberio is said to have thrown people, and the height of the rock at this time only accentuated the depth of the water. I can be brave when people are around; but when I'm alone, telling myself that I'll make it all right doesn't help much. At one time I had a lift—and hope. Going around a rock and passing a clucking cave I thought I'd come to some land, but I had miscalculated the distance. Next, rowing past the White Grotto, I expected to see the Faraglioni and a small settlement of fishermen's houses. But there was not a ship or a house in sight, and there was no place I could get ashore without being dashed against the rocks.

At one spot there is a very small beach, but this was foaming in the tide, and the rocks periodically exposed there had ridges like razor blades. I don't think I have invoked the help of God for myself since the days of childhood. It seemed to me on that stretch of dark travel, with no apparent exit from danger, that finally the bill was being presented to me and the time had come. I once did the scenery for a play called *Noé*, by Obey. Pierre Fresnay played the title role, and toward the last curtain he raised his hands and, looking heavenward, said, "Thank you, dear Lord." I thought of that scene as I kept paddling methodically, and suddenly, with these same words and my paddle held up in both hands, I greeted the sight of Punta Tragara. By that time I sat in several inches of water.

The sea rose and fell as I approached the small landing. The fishermen had taken out all their boats, and now two of them came down and after a great deal of waiting for the right wave to lift the craft close enough to them, they got me and the *sandolini* up on the rock. Before the next wave came they had hoisted me out of the boat.

I was very thirsty, and presently I was on the way to the wonderful Restaurant da Luigi. This place is characteristic of the isle, and here one can see why Capri has not suffered the fate of the Riviera. The Restaurant da Luigi is built on a platform supported by high, slim chestnut trees. Its cover is of straw mats, the chairs as well as the floor seem to be made of old orange crates; it all sways and creaks as you walk, it creaks as you sit down and every time you move it moves with you. The food is fine and the diner is served with a special concern as if he were the guest of the family.

With all its fame, Capri never has been "developed." Nowhere in Capri is there a "casino"—nowhere has anybody done so much as build a pier for guests to go swimming, or even a stairway or a ladder down into the water. The tiny beaches are covered with egg-sized pebbles that hurt your feet, and all except the native fishermen stumble along the shore and into the water with both arms extended to balance themselves.

On top of this, the submerged rocks are covered with sea urchins, a glasslike jet-black kind wearing a bouquet of spines, long, black and sharp and arranged like those of an angered porcupine. When stepped on, the spines break off under the skin, and the exceedingly painful removal of these splinters is an operation as frequent and casual as having cinders removed from eyes in New York drugstores. The sea urchins are most plentiful at the Baths of Tiberio and the Punta Tragara. The bathing cabins are little houses with a bench inside, made by the fishermen, and they are clean. Unless you swim from a boat, the best way to go swimming without pain is to buy tight-fitting rubber shoes—they are especially made for this kind of seashore and are sold in several stores in Capri.

From time to time I hired a 200-pound coachman named Luigi Balsamo. The day I got off the boat in Capri, Luigi was there with other coachmen but he, unlike his colleagues, did not shout for patronage among the debarking passengers. It was raining, and Luigi let his horse eat in peace. In fact, he held an umbrella over it.

The horses here are reasonably well treated; the natives have learned that tourists don't like them to use the whip. Also, the horses have no bits but instead, a light, loose metal brace, sometimes cushioned with lamb's wool. The brace is placed over the horse's nose, the reins are attached to two bars that extend left and right. Wagon and gear are kept shined and polished, and the horses are washed and rubbed every day. Into the harnesses on top of their heads are stuck flags, feathers, or brightly colored artificial flowers.

On one drive Luigi took me to the famous Villa San Michele, an eyesore inside and

out. It was built by the author of *The Story of San Michele,* Dr. Axel Munthe, a man
Luigi, having sometimes driven him about, remembered well. Luigi quoted the one
German phrase the doctor (a Swede) was fond of: *"Gute Reise,"* a contraction of "I
wish you a good trip"—a way of saying goodbye. Disliking German tourists on Capri,
the only pleasure the doctor felt about them was to wish them goodbye.

The house of Luigi stands at the end of a narrow street in Anacarpi. At the end of a
day his horse is put into the clean and warm stable on the ground floor of the house,
where he is covered with a blanket and fed his hay. Upstairs the family sits down to
spaghetti *Milanese*—eight pounds of it every night. With it they drink a good Capri
wine, the real one. I told Luigi what a wonderful life he led.

"Ah, signore, Luigi knows it," he said, his family smiling confirmation.

The day I left Capri, Luigi took my baggage and me down to the ship. He wanted,
in the fashion of Italians, to be especially nice to me. He pulled out a handkerchief,
dabbed his eyes and, shaking both my hands, he said to me on account of my accent,
"Auf Wiedersehen" and—*"Gute Reise."*

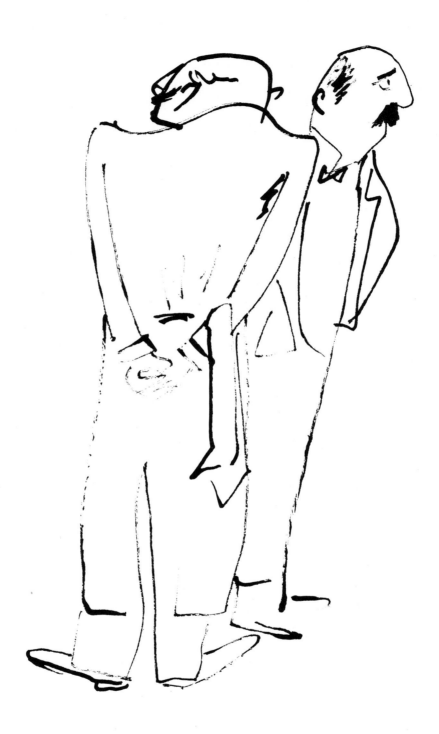

CINDERELLA ISLE, ISCHIA

THE HEAD PORTER of the Quisisana, which is the Waldorf-Astoria of Capri, is a person any casting director would immediately dress in the toga of a Roman senator, consul or even an emperor. With the dignity that behooves such a figure, he came from behind his desk, threw up both arms and, closing his eyes, said, "If you want to see Ischia, take a yacht and go there and float around it. But Ischia—I warn you—the natives there are indifferent if not rude to visitors, and there is not one good hotel on the island. Somewhere there are two sisters named Pirozzi, or something, who cook in their home, but first of all you must know them, and next you must inform them ahead of time when you will come and how many you will be."

I still asked for the best way to get to Ischia, and he picked up a guidebook by Dottore Cesare Tropes. Its title was *Naples Environs,* and in it were listed:

Cumae	Capri
Herculaneum	Amalfi
Pompeii	Paestum
Sorrento	Capua

"You see, signore, as far as travel is concerned, Ischia does not exist. It is like Africa —if you insist upon going there, you are on your own." With that he went to tie tags on the baggage of a group from Hollywood going back to the security of the Hotel Excelsior in Rome.

I sought out the agent of the American Express Company. "No," he said, "we have no itinerary for Ischia. It is not included in our program, but a boat goes there from Naples." The man from Cook's merely shook his head.

Later, I sat in one of the world's most simple and beautiful restaurants, the Sirene, on the shore at the Marina Piccola. At a small table on my left sat a couple with whom I had a nodding acquaintance. Formerly Italians, they lived in America and had come here for a vacation. They were speaking in English, and each held a menu.

Husband: "You take the spaghetti?"

Wife: "You take the spaghetti. I—no. If I eat the spaghetti, soon I cannot get into that new bathing suit and half my charm is gone."

She studied the menu for a while, then ordered the spaghetti anyway. The spaghetti eventually came and she took off her sunglasses and said, "I just want to have a look at these beautiful spaghetti before I eat them." She put the sunglasses on again and ate the full oval platter of spaghetti—it must have been about two pounds.

I had a *languoste,* which is the European crayfish. It looked good but it had a very strong iodine taste, stronger than the usual iodine taste of shrimps, for instance. The proprietor asked me how I liked it, and I answered that I preferred lobster to crayfish, that I thought Maine lobster was the best in the world, and that the *languoste* in Italy, on account of the warmth of the water, was not as good as the kind one gets in France. At the table to the right of me sat an Italian, also of the Roman emperor type—who resembled a statue of Julius Caesar in a museum in Naples. He looked down his nose

SANTANGELO ISCHIA.

64   at the *languoste* he was eating and cleared his throat—he was obviously displeased with my remarks about the quality of Italian crustaceans, and I knew he was preparing a speech.

A fisherman leaned over the banister that separated the restaurant from the stair leading to the beach, and I asked him how long it would take him to sail me to Ischia. About four hours was the answer. The proprietor of the Sirene came to the table with his wife, and said, "Oh, you're not thinking of going to Ischia—not for any length of time."

I said that I would like to spend some time there.

At this, Big Caesar could contain himself no longer. He dropped his fork and the last leg of the *languoste*. "For heaven's sake," he said, "don't go—you would die there. Take my advice and stay away." He washed his fingers and wiped his lips; he put the napkin down and turned his magnificent head toward me.

"Listen," he went on, "I have lived in America for years—I go there every winter. My sister has an apartment on Park Avenue—at an insane price, of course. Imagine, last year she paid one hundred and twenty-five dollars just to have one chandelier hung." He stopped to look at his audience. There was the proprietor, who had worked several years in a spaghetti joint owned by his brother in Jersey City; there was the proprietor's wife; seated near the kitchen was an elderly English gentleman with a young friend; then, a group of six—an Italian family from Naples; and the two people on my right. Big Caesar addressed his words to all these, rather than to me.

"Oh, I know it so well—that great country, and there are many things that are wonderful about it. But Americans don't know how to live. Take restaurants. Americans always demand a certain ennui, not a place to eat; a hole without air, badly lit, small, and too hard to get in—that is the most important part of a successful place in New York. Not food, not wine, just make it hard to get in so that to obtain a table at all is a mark of distinction. A kind of detective stands at the door and when he nods his head you are in. The hole is known as a 'swell place.'" He imitated the New York pronunciation of "swell place."

Everybody had stopped eating to listen to him, and he continued: "Next, the Americans like to be served by an arrogant waiter—they think that too much attention or servility is undemocratic. The restaurant keeper believes the same—he is never in his kitchen, but busy being democratic, shaking hands, calling people by their first names, kissing the women and slapping the backs of the men. The food we won't discuss." He turned to me: "What you said about American lobster is right, I grant you. But then—try to spoil lobster. It's like prunes. Who can spoil prunes?"

He turned back to his audience and said with mock praise, "Here in Italy we have made every effort to please the traveling public. Great care has been given to establish 'swell places' all over the country, complete with bad waiters and with swing music blowing on the food. The American tourist will find himself at home from Milano to Taormina but never in Ischia, for on that island is still comfort, the real old-fashioned comfort. It's a private place with modest charges and excellent hotels and restaurants; it's the Italy of Italians. There are a few English who live there and like it, but they are too few to spoil it"—I lifted my hand, but he kept on—"I don't say that all Americans are like that. But of those who come to Italy, only a handful has the courage to visit Ischia and maybe one of them has a taste for that kind of place. That one, of course, is richly rewarded."

The next morning Carmine, the fisherman, got his small boat ready, and we sailed for Ischia.

The island of Ischia has always played a Cinderella role. When the Emperor Augustus saw Capri, he traded Ischia to the Neapolitans for Capri, though the former is five times as large. Since then Capri has become famous, while Ischia still belongs to the natives. It has no tourist trade, and, despite the words of Big Caesar, there are no good hotels. It is, as the chief porter said, in parts as savage as Africa, and, as the other man observed, it is private. The people, if not unfriendly, appear indifferent to the visitor; there is no great comfort in sleeping or eating, unless you are invited to the houses of friends who live there. It is a place of great interest and is scenically as magnificent as Capri. If you suffer from arthritis you will find it probably the most wonderful place on earth—the hope against hope.

Ischia, the largest island in the Gulf of Naples, is volcanic, and on it are many natural hot springs. The Italian naturalist Tenore determined that these volcanic wells protected the plant life of the island during the glacial period when the rest of Europe's vegetation was destroyed. Today this vegetation is so varied that Ischia seems like a cramped encyclopedia of all the world's flora. Plants of the tropics thrive here, plants that are usually found only in the West Indies, Arabia, Central Africa and India.

The island is dominated by the bulk of Monte Epomeo which, along with other local mountains, is the result of ancient volcanic upheavals. The immense ash and lava deposits of Epomeo make plant growth as lush as it is on Vesuvio. In 1850 a forest of pines was planted on the largest of the tufaceous masses, the *Lava dell' Arso*, which ran down Monte Epomeo into the sea. The forest still stands today.

If the coloration of the rock along the coast of Capri is astonishing and bright, here it is of more subtle, softer shades; yet the landscape changes from the tame and idyllic to sudden savagery. While you are afraid to walk fast in Capri for fear of coming to the ends of it, here you can stretch your legs. While in Capri every road, every house and garden, every face becomes known to you in a few days, here is space and surprise, and the people lose themselves in foliage and on sandy beaches. The existence of the people of Ischia is simple; here is still the patriarchal pattern of life. After a while one finds out that the natives are shy rather than indifferent.

The visitor may take part in the sorrows and joys of the people, but he will never disturb them by his presence or cause them to change their ways. For example, there are no feasts, native dances or local celebrations arranged for the benefit of the tourist, as in Capri. The men, with the exception of a few shopkeepers and government officials, are fishermen or peasants. The women repair nets or they are busy making straw baskets for wine bottles or for hanging cheese. The straw comes from Monte Epomeo. Almost all the girls of Lacco Ameno are called Restituta, that being the name of the saint of the whole north coast. This remarkable saint, according to legend, arrived from Africa on a floating millstone. The fishermen of Lacco Ameno waded out and took her ashore, and every year starting on May fifteenth the event is celebrated for three days with a regatta of fishermen's barques.

The women of the interior of the island, most of whom stay on Ischia all their lives, are nymphlike creatures of great beauty. They are devoted to flowers, a characteristic relatively rare in the south of Italy; they have lovely voices, which is even more unusual. They also have large eyes, even larger than those of their sisters on the mainland.

The young men have less to recommend them, and in the interior they are said to be hostile toward outsiders. A German historian I met on the island, Baron Eckehardt von Schacht, said that their attitude is explained by their history; the islander's experiences with visitors have made him suspicious.

Since the fall of Rome, Ischia has been attacked, occupied and pillaged almost without interruption. The Saracens began it in 813, followed by the Pisans in 1135, after which pirates took over; next came the Germans under Henry VI and Frederic II, followed by the Angevins. All these conquerors left their imprint on the native population so that you see today a mixture of Nordic, Arabian and Spanish strains. Under the Spanish occupation of Alfonso I, all the male population of the island was abruptly sent away and men of Catalonia brought in, and the women and maidens were forced to marry them. The frequent Spanish family name Pattalano is evidently derived from Catalano. In 1545, the Corsican pirate Barbarossa kidnaped four thousand additional Ischian men and sold them into slavery. Unlike the Spaniards, he did not replace them with Corsicans. There was also much infiltration from Arabia and Morocco during that time.

In addition to invasions, the islanders suffered the terrors of earthquake and of the volcano which was in constant eruption, taking thousands of lives.

Under the pressure of these conditions many of the peasants took to the sea, and there developed in Ischia a type of tough fisherman who still sails small boats to the far fishing grounds of Sardinia, and carries cargoes of wine to France, Spain and the north of Italy. Also, the local boatman is skilled at catching forty winks while the noonday sun is hottest.

In 1580 an ancient medico, philosopher and scientist named Iasolini published a book in which the mineral wells of Ischia were endorsed in the delirious vein of a public relations counsel of our day. The text of this prospectus is here translated word for word:

If your eyebrow falls off and you lose the hair on your eyelids as well, go and try the baths of Piaggia Romana.

Are you unhappy about your complexion? You will find the cure in the waters *di Santa Maria del Popolo*.

Are you deaf? Then go to the *Bagno d'Ulmitello*.

Blind? Then immediately go to the *Bagno delle Caionche*. Have you headaches, liver or kidney trouble? Take yourself to the *Bagno di Fontana*.

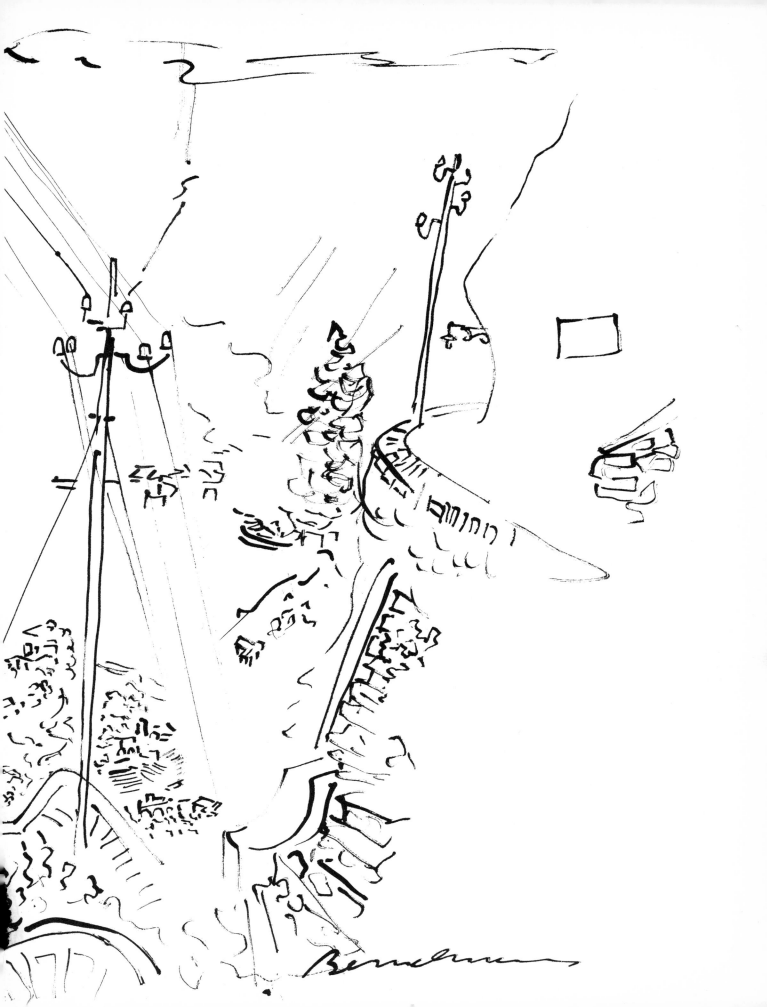

If you know anyone who is getting bald, anyone who suffers from elephantiasis, or another whose wife yearns for a child, take the three of them immediately to the *Bagno di Vitara;* they will bless you.

How much the followers of Iasolini benefited is not known. There are, however, in the National Museum of Naples, a number of votive tablets dating from the Greek period and bearing words of thanks for miraculous cures.

The most frequented baths are on the north side of the island and are fed by a

ISCHIA

spring named Gurgitello, from which source flow every day seven hundred thousand liters of hot water.

In the neighborhood of Casamicciola is the most famous spring on the island, **the Terme Restituta.** This well is of the highest radioactivity known, having been measured at 376 Mache units. The person who came to Ischia and discovered this fact, unknown until the twenties, was Madame Curie. The next most radioactive spring in the world is at Bad Gastein, in Austria, and measures only 149 Mache units.

The baths on the north coast of Ischia are formal. Some of them have classical

façades and remind one of European spas; on the south coast of the island there are just as many hot springs, but all are primitive. If one walks along the beach from Sant' Angelo toward the east, one will occasionally hear an anguished moan coming from the interior of the earth; farther on, the beach emits steam as if the skin of the earth were thin as paper. A hand extended over this surface is pulled back immediately; a kettle of fish can be cooked in this sand in a few minutes. But close to the sea it is cool enough for the natives to take steam baths in pools scooped in the beach.

Walking on, one comes to a narrow ravine which widens into a cave with perpendicular walls; it is called the Valley of the Violet Rays, or the Obscure Cave. As in the Blue Grotto on Capri all is blue and silver, so here every object is said to appear in violet light. Upon visiting it I noticed no such phenomenon—the light was plain daylight.

In a ravine rather than a cavern lies the oldest bathing establishment on the island. It is prehistoric in point of age, as well as in manner of operation. It is open to speculation with what instruments and by whom the bathing cabins were hewn into the rock. Your privacy is assured by a girl named Restituta, who hangs up a large cloth with the texture of a soggy dishtowel. Behind this you undress and put your clothes on a stone block; then you step into the bathtub which, like the cave, is cut out of lava rock. In a loud voice you announce if you want any change in the temperature of the water. According to your directions, Restituta directs hot or cold water toward your tub by the most primitive means—a system of channels hewn into stone.

To the southwest, in back of Lacco Ameno, where the street leads over a pass across weathered lava, the landscape takes on a character equaled only in Africa; the illusion is supported by the architecture of the houses, which stand far apart. The people are very friendly and hospitable. Near Forio, an engaging and prosperous town of six thousand, whose houses are also of African design, begins the zone in which Ischia wine grapes are grown; the vineyards reach south, all the way to Panza, a distance of about two miles. The grapes ripen in glowing heat, the beaches are wide, covered with volcanic sand, and the land is watered with warm mineral springs. Here tomatoes ripen in April, to be exported to Naples and Rome. The specialty of the small village of Panza is a wine called *Sorriso di Panza,* which translates into "The Smile of the Stomach." It is sweet, and not everybody's drink.

To come upon a new horizon unexpectedly and find a view which would be described as "breath-taking" in a guidebook, is as great a discovery as finding a real Van Gogh in a junkshop. Of such astonishing surprise is the view that suddenly unfolds as you leave the magnificent, ancient and dirty town of Panza.

Nearby, the land is like an immense amphitheater, with thousands of steps descending to the sea. The steps are in reality man-made terraces on which corn, figs, wheat, grapes and olives grow. Deep stone cleavages framed in the red of poppies lead down to where the arena would be. In the exact center of the picture stands the Torre Sant' Angelo on a towering peninsula.

From this point starts the trip to Ischia Ponte (an alternate name for Ischia), the principal town on the island.

The hottest and most crowded bus I have ever been in takes the traveler on a road like a roller coaster. The saint whose job it is to protect autobuses on Ischia deserves the most beautiful niche and fresh flowers every day. Nowhere do people depend on saints as they do here; curves are taken blindfolded and at top speed, and if the curve is downhill, the pull of gravity is happily added to the motor's best efforts. The driver talks with his hands to a friend sitting beside him, waves at colleagues on other buses— and nothing happens. Along this route appear vineyards from which comes the wine that is sold as Capri wine. It is good wine and its origin could be admitted without shame, but the power of labels here is as strong as it is anywhere else. After passing the vineyards we come to the pine forest on the *Lava dell' Arso*, and to Ischia Ponte, the seat of the Bishop of Ischia. The Bishop, a very round little man, crosses frequently to Naples. And as he walks the deck, blessing everyone who greets him, green and golden threads hang from his hat and wave in the breeze.

The landmark of Ischia, high on a narrow rock and visible for miles, is the Castello. It was built by Alphonso V of Aragon about 1450 and later occupied by the Syracusans, who fled the island during an earthquake. Subsequently the poetess Vittoria Colonna, an admirer of Michelangelo, lived there. Now the fishermen of Ischia Ponte hang their nets there to dry. It's exactly like the castle you see when you close your eyes and imagine a castle on a rock.

In this already varied and interesting place, the harbor of Porto d'Ischia is an added curio, being the only harbor of its kind in the world. It was originally a landlocked crater lake, situated close to shore. In the 1850's a passage was cut from the lake to the sea, an undertaking which took two years and resulted in the safest harbor in the Gulf of Naples. Here are found the classic coastwise sailing boats, still rigged with colored sails; their cargo is wine, fruit and vegetables.

Near this unique harbor is a small park and in the park is a bench which had a part in altering one of the traditions of the island. On the morning of July 17, 1943, a man sat on that bench gazing toward the sea, contemplating the beauty of his land, his new freedom, and the truth of the proverb that the mills of the gods grind slowly. Suddenly he was dead—and from that day on, the people of Ischia have considered their unluckiest number to be not thirteen, but seventeen.

The man's name was Lucetti. As a youthful anarchist he had had the courage to toss a bomb at Mussolini's car. The bomb struck the car's hood, bounced to the top and rolled off without exploding. Lucetti was caught and sent to Ponza, where he was imprisoned for seventeen years until the Allied troops liberated him. He reached his home on the island of Ischia on July 17, walked to the bench and sat down. And there he was killed by the last shell fired from Procida by the Germans.

During my stay on Ischia I made the acquaintance of Professor Georgio Buchner, who lives in Porto d'Ischia, and who guided me to places and people the less fortunate

visitor never sees. But he did not guide me to the restaurant of the Sisters Pirozzi, at Ischia Ponte. I found that happy establishment on the tip halfheartedly given me by the head porter of the Quisisana, at Capri. At the Sorelli Pirozzi I ate my 10,000th kilometer of spaghetti, and I can only say that it was as good as the best I have eaten in all of Italy. It was not necessary to obtain a formal introduction to the sisters, as the head porter had said, nor was I required to reserve a table in advance—all the dishes are cooked to order. And the prices are extremely reasonable. So frugal is the life of the savant that when I mentioned this meal to Professor Buchner, he said, "So-so-h'mmm—you had dinner last night at the Sorelli Pirozzi. Tell me—is it really as elegant as people say it is?"

"Have you never been there, Herr Professor?"

"No. Never."

"How long are you on this island?"

"Oh, approximately forty years."

"And you never get tired of it?"

"Never. You know it is incredible, but after forty years of taking walks I can still discover new ones."

Naturally, we ate at the Sorelli Pirozzi that night, in Ischia exclusiveness.

As everywhere in Italy, uncounted saints are revered on Ischia, every one of which has his feast day. Every village has its own patron saint, and all of them are carried about in processions with singing, candles, flowers and much rivalry.

During the big earthquake of 1883, the patron saint of Porto d'Ischia earned immense gratitude and praise. While there were thousands of dead on other parts of the island, and the neighboring town of Casamicciola suffered total destruction, not even a floor tile was loosened in Porto d'Ischia. The poor citizens do everything to make the feasts of this saint glorious, and spend a good deal of money on spectacular fireworks.

The favorite song of the island is dedicated to St. Restituta; it is old but ever new, and it goes:

> *Oh, holy Restituta, thanks to thee*
> *The beans have grown,*
> *The quail are gone*
> *And so at last has the enemy.*

There is also a limerick left behind by a visiting poet scribbled on a washroom wall. At least it tells one how to pronounce "Ischia."

> *An Englishman living on Ischia*
> *Got gayer and fatter and friskier.*
> *Between dancing jigs*
> *And stuffing on figs*
> *He drank gallons and gallons of whiskia.*

THE ROAD TO SALERNO

It's wise to get an Italian to drive you from Naples to Salerno, as he will anticipate the donkey caravan, the children playing in the street, the parked car of the tourist around the next tight bend. The beginning of this trip is not inspiring—we hasten first along a road that reminds you of the Pulaski Skyway or any such passage through the part of a large city that is given to factories, piers, warehouses and freight yards. The scene improves at Portici and at Resina, the station of the Vesuvian funicular. Portici and Resina stand on the ruins of Herculaneum, which, together with its plebeian sister-town Pompeii, was destroyed by the eruption of A.D. 79. The antique city of Herculaneum lies at present about twenty meters below the new towns.

We come to Torre del Greco, souvenir and coral jewelry town, after some driving in scenery that is less pleasant than a ride through the Pennsylvania countryside. The road goes upward to Boscotrecase and Casabianca, and the enchantment is still to come. We also pass Torre Annunziata, distinguished as the center of the macaroni and canned fruits industry.

At Valle di Pompei is the Sanctuary of Santa Maria del Rosario, a church with an uninspired modern façade, but containing a wonder-working picture of the Madonna, with the rosary.

Beyond Valle di Pompei we see fields of cauliflower, artichokes and tomatoes. The world here is still plain, and lined with the soft greens of chestnut trees and filbert bushes; forests lie along the hills. Hereabouts countless springs—most of them benevolent and warm—run unused into the sea. By way of Vico, one turns past the Punta di Scutolo and arrives at the point where magnificence begins—the plain of Sorrento is before you.

There are arguments about Sorrento, and people hold that other places further along the road are more magnificent; it's like arguing whether the sunrise or the sunset is more beautiful. Sorrento lies in a magic garden, and most of its hotels perch at the edge of high cliffs.

Along here stood the house in which the poet Torquato Tasso lived. The house fell into the sea together with the ground on which it stood. Near that spot is the villa of my companion Mariano.

Its garden is immense—in fact, it's a romantic park rather than a garden. It is filled with orange trees, and the oranges fall all night, plop-plop, to the ground. Here, as in all the orange gardens of this region, one finds the tall slim poles supporting cross-trees.

The arrangement is curious, and best illustrated if we imagine a potted geranium protected by darning needles stuck upright in the earth and tied together so as to form a loose square cage about the plant. The device covers the whole park, and on top of the structure at regular intervals are small huts made of sticks and straw, in which straw mats are kept. When cold and wind threaten the fruit, the people climb like acrobats up to this immense latticework and attach the mats to the reedy structure; it sways visibly sometimes, but it holds together and gets the oranges through cold spells.

The oranges of Sorrento are bitter and small and would never get to market in America. The trunks of the orange trees are sometimes eaten and hollowed, but bear as well as those with solid trunks. Mariano's orange garden is lined with palms, beyond which is an ancient balustrade—and a sudden descent of several hundred feet down to the sea. From here you may see Vesuvio, Naples and Capri, and it has been written about the place, "See Sorrento and die." There is always singing in the garden, and you will find in shady places under the trees young girls with garden shears, busy trimming the thin top branches of the orange trees. In one part of the property stands a mill for pressing olive oil, its mechanism as ancient as the Bible. A lot of grapes grow along here, as well, and Tiberius is said to have preferred Sorrentine wine above all others.

If ever you have seen the apricots ripen along the foot of Vesuvio, and observed the violence of the blossoming trees; if the warm perfumed air that rises has made you groggy, then you will understand this wine. It is out of the volcanic earth, it's not a wine with a bouquet, it is too insistent; it's a strong wine, a good wine.

Voltaire has said that man is the only animal that drinks when it is not thirsty, that laughs, and that makes love the year round.

Everyone who comes here takes easily to wine. Look at someone and he smiles—you hear laughter in every street, and the babies seem to fall out of trees as the oranges do in Mariano's garden. Also, I have never seen a child cry in Capri, in Ischia or anywhere along this road.

Disregarding the de luxe hotel, there are no more desolate restaurants anywhere than those along the road up to Sorrento. We stopped at one, of a degree of dreariness hard to match. Its interior was painted the color of mud, and garlands of artificial grape leaves hung down the cords of the six cloudy bulbs that barely lighted the place. On the walls were pictures of the road from Naples to Positano, art distinguished by a particularly bad eye for line and color, but not humorous, as such decorations often are. The water in the pictures was a stagnant green, the houses a dingy brown, and the only comprehensive thing about them was the proprietor's explanation that his brother, a professor of painting, had executed them.

I sat still on a black cane-bottom chair, but Mariano, with an elaborate show of appreciation and with the great kindness of Italians, followed the proprietor into another room to see more of the same brushwork. I tasted the wine in the meantime. It was of the Sorrentine quality and very good. I listened to a girl speaking English with a German accent at the next table, and to her companion, a man who spoke German with an American accent. The pair had just come from an excursion to Capri.

"Vell, so I didn't imachine it atall, Chohnnie," said the girl. The American asked what was wrong with it. "But I heard about all the *eleganz*," said the girl, "and the hotels. When I think about Berlin—the Adlon, the Fürstenhof, the really elegant hotels we had—vell, I don't think that what I've seen so far is very *grossartig*, or *wunderbar*, and places like this—*mein Gott*—I have to force the food down, it's all so filthy. These lazy Italians . . . I must say—I'm not very impressed."

Back at the hotel that night, I opened my old travel book on Italy and read Gregorovius, who visited Italy in 1853. I translate

Here let us sit at the edge of a chestnut forest between myrrh bushes and look at the land before us . . . here are golden-blond muscatel grapes that are made transparent by the sun, here the white, pure grape from which the *vino buono* is made; all the grapes are heavy, and each is faultless; beyond are fields of Turkish corn, and olive trees. In this terraced landscape framed by stone walls, each foot of land is cultivated.

Can one believe that here in the center of such plenty, the peasant is poor? Looking over this terrain, one would assume it to be El Dorado, lived in by the happiest of people—yet, as you walk through this paradise, the people you meet all wear the look of hunger, of misery. All these fruits one gets for nothing do not supply a living for the native. He would starve to death were it not for corn meal, which is the staple of his existence. The cause for the misery is in the agrarian conditions . . . The farmer owes a fourth of his income as rent to the landowner—in this case, Prince Colonna. It is the old curse of latifundia that impoverishes the people. Usury knows no bounds; even from the poorest, ten per cent is taken.

In the case of bad crops—and they often follow year after year—the farmer drowns in debt. If he borrows money or grain, the interest ruins him, the rich and the cloisterers wait for his ruin, until at their own price they acquire his property and he becomes their vassal and workman. I have had much opportunity to observe these conditions and as a rule the process is as follows:

First, the debtor sells the ground, but the trees (*gli alberi*—which means also the grapevines) remain his, for the time being, and continuing to care for them he also

TRISTE MOUTARDE

Political EDIFICE

continues in his indebtedness. Soon he offers to sell the trees as well as the ground, and now he is completely the tenant farmer—he and his family are in bondage.

He sells his wine—for himself he uses the second pressing. He needs bread—wheat is much too costly; he eats *polenta,* buying or planting Turkish corn. All the natives eat *polenta,* as a kind of meal or as cake—as such it is known as *pizza.* When you meet someone on a road and ask him what he ate for breakfast, he answers *pizza,* and what will you have tonight? *Pizza.* The yellow corn paste is cooked in the form of a pancake on a flat stone over coals and eaten very hot. The family sits in a circle enjoying this meal. With it they sometimes eat salad, and in high times there is oil to season the salad; occasionally there is a watery soup made of vegetables, chicory and other herbs. Wine stimulates nervous energy, but it doesn't nourish; one can imagine then, with what excitement the people look toward the harvesting of the corn.

Toward the end of July, the ears form, and then the plant needs rain. If none falls and the incessant sun scorches the fields, the people become afraid and the daily processions start in the late afternoon to beg the saints for rain. Near madness, the women scream *"Grazie, grazie Maria"* as Saint Anthony is carried through the fields. The monks gesticulate . . .

Later, sitting with Mariano on a rock in this same landscape, discussing Gregorovius and the poverty of the Italians, I asked, "Is it still the same?"

"Well, more or less so, yes," he said. He also explained that the *pizza* we know is a bonbon—a de luxe creation—compared to the *pizza* the peasants make of *polenta.*

The first impression of Positano is peculiar. One arrives on top of the city and sees it below, in a semicircle. Wherever you go in the city you must go up or down, and your first days in Positano cause you acute pains in your legs. I called on a friend who was not at home, but a neighbor said, "Just use your shoulder and the door will open." He had a fixed-up peasant house. The interiors of these houses are delightful, but the beds are awful. They consist of a frame of chicken wire resting on four wooden blocks, and if you sit down carelessly the whole thing collapses beneath you. You sleep in it motionless, with hands folded, like a corpse.

In this part of the country, except in a few select places, the baths and washbasins are also of the most primitive kind. The inhabitants of Positano number about two thousand. Most of them live off fishing; some receive money from relatives who have gone to America, and the tourist season affords an income to others. In this city of stairs there is no weight that the citizens cannot carry on their heads. Pianos, heavy trunks, and even the departed in their coffins are carried to the cemetery balanced on a man's head.

The houses are primitive—one large room with an open fireplace. Several have a sort of Turkish bath in the basement, sunk into the rocks, and it is assumed that these trace back to the Saracens. There is one palace in the town, the entrance to which is a remarkable gate flanked by columns decorated with the heads of Moors. During the Napoleonic wars when one could reach Positano only by vessel, this house was the residence of Prince Murat.

Some sixty artists and writers, most of them of the garret type and as yet undiscovered, live in Positano. About two years ago, a group of Americans bought several houses which they decorated and modernized. In the whole of Positano there is only one cow, and since nothing grows on the rocks, grass is carried down to it from the mountains. High in the mountains are two small villages that supply the town with vegetables, milk, butter, eggs and charcoal. The peasants are obliged to climb up and down several hundred feet a day, heavily loaded.

One is again and again astonished at the cleanliness of the streets and the houses. The combination kitchen-living-room-bedroom is shining, the clothes of the people are spotless and one would never hesitate to sit at table with any of them.

All are filled with a passionate love of children that is returned with an adoration of their parents. When I saw parent talking to child it was always with the attention and intimacy of close friends exchanging important views. Although the people are friendly, to become intimate with them you must have lived in Italy long enough to have shed the tourist's inquisitiveness. Even so, it takes time before they let you come close. They show at the beginning a certain subconscious contempt for the foreigner, and one cannot blame them since most of the visitors do not go to church, or bother to hide excesses and irregularities.

The town's leading restaurant is a café called the Bocca di Bacco—the Cave of Bacchus—owned by the local priest and his five nephews. The latter wait on table, and one of them is a remarkable photographer. To reach the beach from the restaurant, one passes the church and the miraculous Madonna which gave Positano its name. The legend says that in the time of the Saracens devout fishermen brought her from the south, and as they came to the bay on which the present Positano lies, the statue said suddenly: "*Posi—posi—*" (Put me down—put me down). The feast day of this particular Madonna—a large statue weighted down with false jewelry—is in August, and it is surprising that she doesn't ask the fishermen of Positano to take her away during the eight days of uninterrupted celebration with trumpets blaring, constant explosions, drumming, shouting and shooting all night long.

Positano fishermen who have emigrated to Argentina send large sums of money every year to insure the greatest possible glory for this feast. The last evening of the celebration is the high point, and all that the church can contribute in glory and drama is employed—prelates wrapped in clouds of incense, nuns leading children dressed as little monks and angels; also half-naked little cupids symbolizing the bed of love, marching along in the parade with six-year-old bishops in miters. The people are well formed, and, in spite of the many stairs, the girls have handsome legs. The young men pelt the procession with flowers. Rugs hang out of windows, and everything is decorated with the most elaborate artificial flowers.

Slim, black-haired adoring men smile at their girls in recognition; even the prelates and nuns are gay. Everyone wanders happily about, laughing, talking—and then suddenly someone starts a prayer or a hymn. Although hands are folded and voices are raised in holy song, the eyes still rove, and there is always an answering smile through the rain of flowers as the throng wanders, singing, down the steps to the decorated fisherboats. Immediately after the church music, a trumpeter starts an aria from *Aïda* and the orchestra follows his cue. By now the celebration seems to have nothing whatever to do with religion, although there is a good deal of drinking in honor of the Madonna at the Bocca di Bacco, and hours later a torchlight procession is organized again to take her back up to her church. At the stands that sell *pizza* and wine, every boy finds his girl.

It is most remarkable that in all this gaiety, day or night, you will never find grossness. If you see someone staggering, it is usually a foreigner; the Italians retain grace— the most simple fishermen and peasants move with the ease of dancers, they never get rough, or accost one another. They drink the cheapest raw wine and it makes them only happy.

After the Madonna is put back into the church, with her gown covered with paper money the people have pinned there, life continues in the Bocca di Bacco where all of Positano meets. Here is the mayor, son of an aristocratic Neapolitan family—able, friendly, and only twenty-eight years old. Here is the poorest fisherman, and here are

tourists, the wealthy, mingling with a ragged painter who lacks the money to buy paint but has enough to nurse a glass of *Lacrima Christi*.

The view from the restaurant includes three large rocks that lie in the water offshore and are called *Li Galli* (The Cocks). Here is the story of how they got there:

Once upon a time there was a ruler who wanted a castle in a hurry. He found a sorcerer who promised to do the job in three days. The sorcerer was a gourmet and fond of roosters, and as his price he asked the duke for all the roosters in Positano. Upon the order of the duke, all the roosters were requisitioned, slaughtered and sent to the sorcerer—all, that is, except one. It belonged to the daughter of a fisherman and, since she loved it dearly, she hid it in her bed. In the dawn, the workingmen of the sorcerer came flying through the air carrying large rocks for the foundation of the castle and, with the first ray of the sun, the hidden rooster crowed—whereupon the sorcerer declared the contract broken, and the workingmen dropped the rocks into the sea. And that is how *Li Galli* were created.

The end of the celebration is again a scene from an opera. The last one to leave the Cave of Bacchus—a talented young painter, crippled from the waist down—is carried home by the son of the local gravedigger.

The most beautiful hours in this stretch of land are toward evening when the sun rolls down beyond the horizon. It sets the sky aglow and makes liquid fire of the sea. We started at such a time to climb the stairwaylike road upward; and when we came to the restaurant at the top, sky and sea were purple and indigo and out over the waters lay a thin red line. The restaurant seems to hang in the sky.

Mariano and I, finding no tables unoccupied, picked one on the cliffside at which a couple sat. The man had the thin, responsible face that one finds among American scientists. As he talked he moved his hands as if examining an imaginary vessel of extreme delicacy. His companion was an Italian girl of the most serious type, and as he spoke to her she held her head a little inclined toward him. It was getting dark, the wind brushed over the sea, and it was now like sitting on the prow of a ship that silently sailed into the night.

Sweet, heavily perfumed air floated the body as well as the mind. The wine, in bottles without labels, was easy to drink. A robust woman carried in a large platter of rice with chicken, olives, mussels and tomatoes; from below came the laughter of the people of Positano and then the ringing of the church bell.

The couple we sat with had refused wine; instead, they sipped the local mineral water and looked completely happy. The young man was again molding his invisible vessel as he talked about Italy and his love for the land and the people. He introduced himself as a Philadelphian, the Roman correspondent for a North American publication. The girl called him Tom.

Several feet away from us was a round metal table surrounded by a group of young Italians, all handsome and elegant. They were gay, and after a while there were as many bottles as people at the table.

The abstemious correspondent at my right asked Mariano something about population and matters political, and then the couple were served a fish so beautiful that it should have been in an aquarium rather than on a platter. The two ate silently, washing the fish down with the benevolent bubbling water—a hard thing to watch. When the entrée was gone, they ate artichokes and then had some tea which, in this area, is abominable. The man sipped his tea from the end of a hollow-shafted spoon, his Adam's apple traveling up and down with each swallow. At last he put down the spoon. For a while he looked as if he were worried, but finally he seemed to find the words for what he wanted to say. I thought it would be about love, and it was.

"Teresa," he started, hesitantly, and then he began his molding again. With determination, as if he were composing an editorial, he continued: "The Italians are the most misunderstood people in the world. The Italians are not lazy, they are not liars, they are not cowards and thieves—I am going to say that over and over again until people will believe it."

"Thank you, thank you," said an Italian who had sat down with us. At the round table there seemed to be a commotion. All the young elegants looked our way and then stuck their heads together and talked excitedly.

The conversation at our table changed to other themes. The patrons of the round table walked out of the terrace and the bottles were cleared away. We paid, and together with the American started the descent, passing from housetop to housetop until, suddenly, under a street lamp, we saw the group which had sat at the round table.

One of the young men, in a state of maniac elation, detached himself from the rest. With eyes glaring and face flushed, he suddenly ran toward the American, slapped his face and challenged him to a duel. The American stood there frozen, looking exactly the way one should when unexpectedly slapped in the face. By the time anyone had realized what had happened, the young man had turned and disappeared with his group. It was like a scene in a play.

The next morning the formalities were carried further in Positano; the challenge was properly presented, with emissaries going from one hotel to the other.

The explanation for the incident is simple. The soft, warm wind had miscarried the word *not*. All the Romans at the round table were sure they had heard the American, say: "The Italians are lazy, they are liars, they are cowards and thieves—and I am going to say that until people will believe it."

"This is very serious," said the girl. "The young man is of the Roman aristocracy, he has challenged you. If you do not accept the challenge your situation in Rome is impossible, for everyone will scorn you. Also, the Roman would be doubly insulted if we gave him the true explanation—he'd think you a coward. What is there to do?"

In the end the correspondent composed a letter which may well serve as a model in such difficult cases. This is how it went:

My dear Prince ——:
    Last night you slapped my face. You were somewhat under the influence of alcohol, and I was too astonished at the time to react. I presume that the slap was part of the procedure of challenging me to a duel.
    I am an American, and since duelling has been out of fashion in my country for many years, my lack of proper training prevents my accepting your challenge. I suggest, however, two ways of settling this matter. First, I shall give a small dinner at the restaurant where we ate last night, and I herewith invite you to attend. When you reach the state of intoxication of last night, I shall return your slap and explain the matter to you, and after that I hope we shall shake hands.
    If this suggestion is distasteful, then I offer an alternative. I shall go into the street and look for you, and when I find you, I will do my best to beat the hell out of you.
    I hope you will accept for dinner, at about eight. Bring anyone you like.

Sincerely,

(signed)

There was a great deal of speculation all day, but around seven the prince climbed the steep road upward. As he entered the restaurant, the American walked toward him and extended his hand. The prince grasped it.

92   "Ah, I am glad," said Mariano. "It seldom ends so nicely. Usually it is hopeless, and you stand there in the morning fog outside Rome." He shivered and drew his coat around himself. "The Americans are changing everything in this world," he said, with a little sadness in his voice.

MIGHTY VESUVIO

94   In the back of a closet in New York, for years I kept a pair of shoes, old but never worn. They were made for me by a Swiss cobbler. They are as formless as a newborn pup and of a mean shade of egg yellow that has refused to change for the better, although I have polished them many times. Over the years, as I have smeared dark cream on them, the right one has turned the shade of a ripe persimmon, the other a screaming red like a Chinese lacquer. Even exposing them to the elements did not improve them, but they were too expensive to throw away.

"In Italy you can wear them and nobody will pay any attention," said a much traveled friend, so I packed them. And then I found to my regret that Italians are very particular about their boots, insist that they fit like gloves and be of simple design. I should have said, however, that the multicolored cloppers were made especially for walking in the high mountains. They had soles as thick as a club sandwich and iron caps at the heels and tips of the soles. All things work out eventually, and now I am glad that I ordered them from Mr. Molnar, *Schuhmachermeister*, 22 See-Strasse, Zurich. Their day finally came—I decided to wear them for the ascent of Vesuvio.

My Italian friend Mariano, who came with me, usually shakes hands whenever he greets me and inquires how I slept. But that day, in the lobby of the hotel in Naples, he stood back without offering his hand. He looked down and said with true Italian politeness, "What a sensible pair of shoes for the volcano, *amico*—how foresighted— *andiamo*, let's go."

"Do I need an overcoat?"

"Yes, and also a sweater."

In the car on the *autostrada* that leads to Portici, Torre del Grecco and Resina, I shifted position and crossed my legs. The left shoe came up like a stop light and my polite companion asked with feigned interest where one could have such a pair of shoes made. And after we discussed the history of them, and of shoes in general, he ended his observations by saying that while they would be very good on Vesuvio, their great value would become apparent to me when climbing Etna or Stromboli. "Vesuvio," said Mariano, "is a promenade compared to the others.

"For the volcano ahead of us," he went on, "we do not have the absolute respect that the Japanese have for Fujiyama; nevertheless, we have an affection for Vesuvio in spite of all the troubles it has caused."

The funicular, built in the '80's, goes to within about a thousand feet of the summit. The famous song "Funiculi! Funicula!" was written about it.

Ascending Vesuvio, the window of the funicular frames for you the most carefully worked out designs for paradise on earth. All the shades of green are here, beginning with the deepest bottle color of palms that stand in shaded spots, progressing to the lighter greens of the foliage of fig, lemon, orange, peach and apricot trees to olive orchards, chestnut forests, and finally to the pallor of the frail leaf and platinum-blond blossoms of the mimosa. The largest fields of light green are those terraced vineyards which produce some of the best wines of Italy. Representative of the region is a white wine called Soma, the Sorrentine wine favored by Tiberio, and a strong wine called Lacrima Christi. This stretch of earth is so fertile that it reminds one of the tropics. The demon Vesuvio, between his outbursts, is a lavish giver. He has covered himself with rich soil and fertilized the land with his volcanic ashes. Here, heaven is below and hell above.

No matter how often you see it, the color of the sea far below delights you; the white hulls of the Capri ships lie on it like billiard balls on green cloth. The houses, painted in pastel colors, would disturb the picture in other latitudes, but here they are proper.

The funicular wobbled over a hump, the clattering of the cogwheels slowed down, and in a pleasant station the trip came to an end.

In contrast to the pink and fat conductor of the funicular was the guide we encountered there. My companion, who loves comfort and came on this trip reluctantly, said, "Look at him, he is at his ease in his role as the devil in the Inferno." The observation was apt, for the man could have played a role in Hades. He was sharp of face, his skin mottled and umber-colored; he wore an American battle jacket and had emerald-green eyes. There were about five other guides in sight, and a sign saying it was unlawful to ascend without a guide. The fellow who approached us, however, acted as if he were the sole custodian of the volcano and attached himself to Mariano and me. In back of him was the observatory, and it was the precise color of my right shoe.

The guide started out with us, carrying the overcoats and camera, and we walked for about fifteen minutes in silence. There was some vegetation—a small pine here, and there a yellow broomflower called *ginestra,* a tough kind of grass; a goat was tethered wherever patches of it appeared.

The volcano itself loses shape as you get closer to it. It is a melancholy scene, and in a little while the muscles at the back of your leg let you know that you are climbing.

"Don't ever speak badly of the Swiss again," said Mariano, and he looked for a rock to sit on, because his feet had begun to hurt. There were now rocks all about of approximately the same size—huge cannon balls with soft surfaces—the ammunition of the volcano.

The guide noticed my shoes and expressed admiration for them. Silently, I apologized to their maker, for they felt as comfortable as slippers. It is a curious thing that in the mountains heavy shoes are lighter to walk in than light ones; these held the foot firmly and gave me a solid stance, which was very important, for not having to worry much about what I stepped on, I could pay attention to the landscape. There were frequent stops now, to catch the breath, and the panorama extended itself more and more. As you turn from the road you find the scene swimming in a violet haze. The vegetation below has moved together into one allover velvety green mantle. There is no sound, no rumbling, no hissing—there is only a soft swish of wind; and this carries to you alternately the scent of lemon and orange blossoms and of roses—and at a shift of the wind, the smell of hell: sulphur oozes up out of cracks and you enter a lunar landscape. You

Saule Pleureuse

Pleureuse

are truly in the domain of Faust. It is worth all the trouble to come here and let this scene surround you—it is grim. On your left is a river as wide as the Hudson at Albany, but it is frozen; its color is indigo, and it drapes itself in astonishing serpentines from high above you down to the right of the observatory. From a distance the stuff of which it is made looks like burnt fat, and you think that when you touch it, it will crumble like old piecrust. But you find it to be as hard as glass.

This is where the real climb began, and here stood a man, all alone in this wilderness, who had the concession of renting sticks to visitors. The sticks were long, made of peeled wood and extremely good to walk with. Now came the ennui of climbing. The guide went ahead, carrying our coats and soon our sweaters too. Often we asked him, "How much longer?" And on we went, following him, staggering along, placing one foot ahead of the other, for the path was now narrow and consisted entirely of slag. I was in reasonable comfort, but Mariano was in misery.

I am used to skiing on dangerous terrain and never experience any vertigo, but the cone of Vesuvio is a frightening place to be and gives you the sensation of walking on the edge of the Empire State Building. There is nothing to keep you from falling in; stone and ashes roll down the outside and the inside of the crater as you walk—or rather, crawl—along it.

You can look down into the crater, but there is no fire or boiling mass of lava visible. Nothing moves except the vapors that rise from both the inside and the outside of the crater. The crater itself, like all immense surfaces that are of one kind of material, changes suddenly with the light that plays on it. One moment it is as static and stony as a moist dungeon, the next, it shimmers as the sunlight passes through a thin cloud, like the milky glass snowballs that are hung on Christmas trees. Direct afternoon sunlight molds it, and then it looks like a herd of elephants imprisoned in mud; it is indigo where the shadows stay, and at the edges of crevasses are strips of yellow light. After we had watched this a while, a cold wind came and I had the sensation of flying. As fast as clouds tear past the windows of an air liner, shreds of vapor rose and were sucked into ravines or swished up over the crater and were twisted into spirals and torn away; at times the crater disappeared from view altogether. As the fogs closed in, the guide warned us not to go out of his sight.

He lit matches, held them close to the ground and they produced a large yellow flame that fed on natural gas in the atmosphere. Then, for a moment, he left us sitting at the edge of the crater, and leaped agilely away through the fog. He returned with a stone, carrying it in a thickly folded newspaper. It was burning through the paper when he reached us.

The guide, probably in an effort to scare us, said that about a dozen Americans who refused guides had fallen into the crater. They had been trying to take pictures and lost their footing. He also told a remarkable story of an Italian who had tried to save the cost of a guide and almost perished. The fellow was a shoemaker's apprentice from Sorrento. He climbed to the crater alone. Emptied by the last eruption, it looked reasonably peaceful and the shoemaker, finding it dull, amused himself by tossing rocks into the mouth of the crater. Heaving a particularly large one, he lost his balance, began to slide, and miraculously caught himself on a small ledge formed by hardened lava. There, hanging over the inner rim, he remained for two days until a guide who came up with a tourist heard his cries. The guide went for help and with the aid of ropes the cobbler was rescued. He was stupefied by the fumes and also in a state of shock, but after a week's hospitalization he returned to Sorrento and was famous from then on. "The moral," said the guide, "is never to go anywhere in Italy without a guide." When he had finished the story, I was very glad that he was there to lead us away from the crater, perhaps to a good restaurant. We stumbled downward in the sulphuric, soupy mist.

As long as volcanoes cook their stone, growling with a bad-tempered rattling of pots and pans—but controlled—they are a safety valve for the fiery core of the planet. And, it has been said, some of them are connected with one another beneath the earth's surface.

Here are some useful products of volcanoes: the mud streams that flow from them harden to form a precious building material. The ashes which are fired into the air for miles and, like the atomic cloud, assume the shape of a mushroom return to earth as one of the best fertilizers known. Volcanic bombs, called *lapilli,* are the slag of brimstone. The product of the highest volcanic activity is lava. A glowing stream of molten stone, it spills over the crater, and, only twenty years after it hardens, it covers itself with a thin layer of greenery which in time becomes the most luxuriant vegetation.

The explosions of a volcano are of a periodic nature, like the tempers of a madman. After he has let off steam, he rests and seems in accord with the world. He is exhausted, the fires are low, and sometimes they go out altogether. In time the crater fills with water, forming a lake that may be of exceptional beauty. The richness of the land attracts people, and whole villages such as we see at the foot of Vesuvio are built from its lava. Suddenly the fire mountain shakes again. In the diary of Vesuvio—since man has kept track of it—there have been about seventy eruptions. At one time, from 1500 on for 131 years, the mountain was so still that trees and bushes covered it and cattle grazed in the crater. In 1631 it exploded again, killing over three thousand people and destroying the surrounding villages with ashes, fire, falling *lapilli* and seven streams of lava. Vesuvio greeted the twentieth century with a tremendous spectacle—a flow of lava that lasted eleven months. It shook the ground and blasted a cloud of ashes thirty-three thousand feet high. By the end of April, 1906, the show stopped as suddenly as it began.

If the ascent to the crater is tiring, coming down is more so; your knees get weak, and at every step you sink ankle-deep into the slag. Soon we reached the place where we had rented the walking sticks, and, turning them in, we walked easier now, back to the broomflowers, the goats and the pines.

"Where do we eat?" asked Mariano, with some enthusiasm.

Close to one station of the funicular is the Hotel Eremo, belonging to
and Son. It is at a height of 1995 feet and the prospectus says that it has
water, fourteen rooms and a magnificent view—unfortunately it was clos
were there. But the observatory was open and the general hellish air that
Vesuvio is present in compact form inside the building. It is the countingh
ter. The walls are decorated with pictures of eruptions and photographs o
fire bombs and the various directors of the observatory. On the desk of the
tor, Professor Imbo, stands an ash tray made of lava. In the vast recesses are
mographs in glass cases recording the mood of the volcano. I asked the you
showed us through this building if the mountain showed any signs of agit
took us to one of the seismographs and showed us the record of the las
needle occasionally had marked periodic tremblings. "Nothing serious.
professor coming downstairs, in the morning," said the young man, pointi
disturbance. And then, pointing at others, he said, "This is the funicular
departing—this was a motorcar—and this is you and your friend." At the
the band, which is about the size of a sling in which one might cradle a bro
a more violent writing, swinging from left to right. "That," said the yo
something far away. Might be an earthquake in Japan or California—b
minor, we won't read about it in the newspapers." The rolls of paper use
activity of the volcano are covered with a film of carbon, and this is done i
fashion. Petroleum is poured into a tiny gutter attached to a handle, and
roll of paper slowly passes over it, picking up soot.

In the basement of the observatory is a room unique in the world—it's li
in an ancient castle. In the center of it, surrounded by a heavy banister
circular platform that stands free and is so constructed that it is level at

In time of great activity, when the whole mountain shakes, a consecr
can stand here and, with his instruments about him in the banister, he is ab
the disturbance going on, the shaking of the very building in which h
about as happy a place as the room in which the electric chair stands.

The observatory, however, stands on a spot that so far has been safe.
have moved past its door, down into the fields, the gardens and the villag
to everything on the way. The lava flows on until, inexplicably, as if some
of pure caprice suddenly gave the order to stop, it halts. "It is," said a nat
chief of a gang of bandits suddenly gave the command to stop plundering
killing, and to fall back into order and form ranks—that's how suddenl
lava stops."

Most of the natives, however, don't mention bandits in connection
They see in it destruction—the evidence of the wrath of God—and ascri
stopping of the lava flow to the powerful intercession of the saints to wh
prayed. The saints, however, are sometimes angered by the avarice of ce
uals. The story is told of a Neapolitan lawyer named Messerante, who h

self an estate on the slope of Vesuvio and spent a good bit of money making it a show place. He entrusted the property to the care of St. Januarius and, over a period of time, spent a good deal of money on celestial insurance.

He built a beautiful chapel for the saint, placing it in the most probable path that a lava stream might take. He bought scented candles and, with his family and servants, frequently prayed at the chapel. During the last (1944) eruption of Vesuvio, the lava stream headed toward the property of the lawyer. There was time to save the furniture and many other treasured possessions. Signor Messerante's employees and neighbors begged him to act and offered to help him, but he refused, explaining that it was the duty of the saint to look after the place. The lava did not stop; it ate up the chapel of the saint and rolled on toward the house. Signor Messerante took the keys to his estate and, with a bitter curse, threw them into the hot liquid as all his property was ruined.

In the middle of the month of August of the year A.D. 79, about six weeks after the coronation of the Emperor Titus, movements of the earth at Vesuvio were observed, but no one thought them dangerous. On the twentieth of August of that year sounds as of distant thunder were heard, and then these signs of upheaval were repeated—yet still no one thought of danger. It is recorded that the birds ceased to sing, cattle became uneasy and bellowed, and all the dogs tore at their chains and barked. The sea was in motion, but only the farmers began to look toward the sky, fearing hail. On the morning of August twenty-fourth, the sky was pale blue and cloudless, the sun shone and it was unusually hot, even for August. Suddenly the earth heaved and from Vesuvio came a deafening explosion. Day turned to night. Lightning struck, and frightened birds that had taken to the air began to fall in a crossfire of burning *lapilli*. Thus began the destruction of Pompeii.

It is told that when Samuel Goldwyn gazed upon the ruins of Pompeii, he turned to a companion and said: "See what happens when people start something and haven't the money to finish it."

All the sayings attributed to Mr. Goldwyn are zestful and apt; so is this one. Pompeii has the air of a classical subdivision gone bankrupt and abandoned. Upon seeing it, the image of grandeur one has had of it is dissolved completely; a homey spirit still lives there. It is very small and sympathetic; it is as if High Tor had spewed lava on a friendly little town like Nyack, New York, or as if Newcastle, Delaware, had suffered an earthquake. Even the most elegant houses in Pompeii are comparatively small, the size of modern American homes. The arrangements of rooms are intelligent. The streets are narrow and the only place of real space is the arena. On almost every street corner is a bar.

On entering Pompeii, the tourist is assaulted by a battalion of guides, not compulsory here. They speak almost every language badly, and the easiest way out is to engage one.

The visitor understands Pompeii immediately—it is logical and simple down to its

102 leaden plumbing, gardens, glassware and cooking utensils. Large blo
were placed at street intersections, so that people could cross without
sandaled feet wet, either in rain water or the refuse usually there. I alway
visiting Roman ruins that we have nothing to match their beautiful baths.

The most interesting part of the ruins was, to me, a set of plaster-ca
of extreme simplicity of line, much like good modern sculpture. The
that were caught in the disaster and calcified. The liquid that encase
even the expressions on their faces. They gasp and reach, twist in agon
open; a mother holds a baby; a couple embrace each other. The forms
articulate as the best in modern sculpture. In one group is a little dog a
of a fox terrier. He appears so lifelike that you wait for him to shift
scratch himself, or get up and run away.

Since Pompeii is small, the visit is not tiring: it is a pleasant walk in the

In a restaurant outside the ruins of Pompeii, I had spaghetti, and I hav
better—although I had had wonderful spaghetti the day before. This ha
again and again. Just as the music fits the landscape here, so does th
the stomach. *Spaghetti Inside* would be a good title for a travel book
find the hard dry wine of Soma to be good also and you don't particul
spots on the tablecloth; you are becoming Italian.

A boy came and offered to shine our shoes. A car filled with Am
arrived. And a man in the garden started to sing "Funiculi! Funicula!"
scene—from the ruins of Pompeii to the table of this restaurant—was
the cone of Vesuvio, which, on a sunny afternoon like this one, is the
shade of lilac. Mariano, my companion, drowsily observed my shoes as th
them. Presently he said, "Please write down for me the address of tha
maker, *amico.*"

The march up and down Vesuvio, the dust of Pompeii and local s
turned my boots—both of them—to the color of eggplants. I looked a
They are old friends—I'll go anywhere with them from now on.